★ ★ ★ WRITTEN BY DESMOND DENTON ★ ★ ★

WILLIAM AUSTEN

DISCOVER THE RIVETING TRUE LIFE TALE

INSPIRED BY THE REAL LIFE STORY OF WILLIAM AUSTEN

WILLIAM AUSTEN

DESMOND DENTON

© 2021 by Desmond Denton. All rights reserved.

No part of this book may be reproduced in any written, electronic, recording, or photocopying form without written permission of the author, Desmond Denton or the publisher.

Published by: ASTORY, Cape Town, South Africa

Interior Design by: Amy Hoffmann

Chapter Artwork by: Emil Weideman

Book edited by: Edward Bennett & Tamzin Atkins

Cover Design by: DESMOND DENTON STORY

ONCE UPON A TIME...

There was a boy who was inspired by telling stories. He lost himself in books so much that he had to start telling the stories with friends via a video tape recorder. He and his friends used to cut together their own movies and handmade title sequences.

He would wake up to see a world filled with drama, conflict, suspense, adventure, and fantasy. It made him feel alive. He would just sit and listen to people and came to this amazing conclusion...

People are moved by emotion and the best emotions are usually engaged by this simple phrase- once upon a time...

He believed that one needs to be training your mind as well as skill. So what did he do next? He started in school working on film sets, from being a runner, making coffee and getting to know the film hierarchy. He studied, worked hard and fell more in love with the film industry. So the next best thing to do was to enroll to the Afda film school where he studied directing and writing. He further has an honours in communication and post graduate in psychology. For the last two years he has won over 16 international awards for is film work and is currently in post production with his apocalyptic tv series Spelonk, set for international release. One of his biggest tests was to take on the 48hour film challenge where they received 12 nominations and 3 awards. This included best film rated by audience review. The boy with dreams, is now an award winning filmmaker who walks with a strong vision of creativity, vision, passion and heart.

This fearless and talented man is... Desmond Denton, International award winning storyteller.

The William Austen story is a film in development by DESMOND DENTON STORY. What started from a conversation has developed into a great friendship between Desmond and William Austen and a heartfelt story of grace, a testimony of God's love to us all.

Contained within these pages is not a story. Rather it holds the confession of a man born into hardship, raised in dire straits and hardened by a life filled with turmoil and abuse. It feels good to be powerful, but at what cost... discover the riveting true life tale of William Austen

DEDICATION

This book is dedicated to the incredible gift of family. Let no man or woman chase after dreams- only to discover the greatest treasure was left behind.

I have been blessed to share life with an incredible woman, Vera, who inspires me to dream and challenges me to make these dreams come alive.

To our children Katelyn, Logan and Robin- you brought about a whole new adventure, a new outlook on life. Thanks for inspiring this dreamer to be even more, and to discover how much there is in the mere everyday moment, right here with you.

TABLE OF CONTENTS

Prologue *1*

Chapter 1 .... *4*

Chapter 2 .... *10*

Chapter 3 .... *18*

Chapter 4 .... *24*

Chapter 5 .... *36*

Chapter 6 .... *42*

Chapter 7 .... *48*

Chapter 8 .... *54*

Chapter 9 .... *64*

Chapter 10 .... *68*

Chapter 11 .... *76*

Chapter 12 .... *84*

Chapter 13: Epilogue *92*

William Austen's Personal Testimony *101*

The book is the prelude for the ministry film we want to produce to impact communities often overlooked

PROLOGUE

The sun was setting near the small coastal townships close to Hermanus, reflecting Golden-Orange rays off the sheeted metal rooftops. As the sun crept down behind the oceanic horizon the town would start to light up, music started pumping in the distance of the Capetonian sprawl as kids played soccer on dusty patches of earth next to the packed city streets. The usual roadside stores dotted the busy intersections, small DIY stalls occupied by all manner of chips; sweets; and cheap cigarettes being tended to by Cape Town's common clay, a foundation built on blue collars. Every other odd stall would have a robust gas-powered grill cooking cheap sausages and onions while the table next was swathed in fruits; vegetables and hotdog roles as well as the few smileys (Pig heads) being sold to the community turning in for the day. One of these vendors was an Old Man, who worked hard with an overweight dog as guard. The passersby and street kids would often take advantage of the elderly. A common occurrence. Today like most days the kids would run past, dirty from soccer, a ball under one arm as they swiped apples and candies from the Old Man's table and ran screaming in glee. He would scream angrily after them: *"Soegah julle Rubbish!" and set his dog on them. This was a fun game for them, being chased by a dog who could barely run and hear the yelling old man. The leader of the pack was the fastest and most arrogant, he turned back and took a bite of apple before yelling back. *"Voetsek, oupa!" The others laughed at this and followed their leader. The old man grumpily called his dog back and sat down on a half-broken crate with a sigh.

Through the crowded streets came a man running as though the Devil himself was nipping at his heels. He was a large man with a shaven head. A bruiser in every meaning of the word. His pace was not towards something. But rather his urgency was to get away from something, or someone. His name is William. Everyone knew of William Austen, a hard man with violence on his resume. His shirt splattered with blood, whose blood was only known to those that chased him. An unsavory group of abalone and drug traders known as the "Numbers". And not far behind him was Ricardo, a tattooed vicious looking colored man. He shoves the boys aside, one of his gang members threw them to the ground desperately chasing after William like a pack of rabid hounds. He turns a corner and pushes himself in an awkward and potentially lethal position. He stood between his pursuers and a High-Wire fence he couldn't scale fast enough. He bends over breathing hard, Ricardo steps into the road, gang members all around. Brandishing knives. His heart beats in his ear like a war drum as he thinks to himself: "What do they say? It's not the size of the dog in a fight, but the size of the fight in the dog. And now the Devil's Dance. It's been like this since the very beginning!"

CHAPTER 1

This is my beginning. This here is how my life started with a drunkard known as my father walked into the hospital with flowers. Shown into the room where I lay still covered in placenta and the cord still attached to my soft belly. My mother Merissa lying there as she looks at her husband. *"Told you I would be here."* Said my father, Paul. My mother smiles for once, the worst is over and her baby boy is born. My father walked over to the Apgar scale where I was being weighed by a pediatrician. The doctor in charge hands him surgical scissors and congratulates him on his fatherhood. He still reeked of booze, taking the scissors and tries real hard to do a neat job of cutting the cord. *"Don't worry now, we have him tied up all nicely."* said the Doctor as a small amount of blood spurted out.

After the Doctor wiped the gunk off me, my father took me in his arms and stumbled over to my mother, placing me in her arms. *"Looks just like his handsome father, doesn't he, Merissa? He scored a whole nine on that test thing."* smiled Paul. *"A whole nine! He really is a winner."* answered Merissa as she touched my tiny hand with her fingers. *"What should we call him?"* my father asked. Merissa looks at her little boy and smiles weakly: *"William"*. *"My little William boy."* My father stated proudly. The next day he arrives a little soberer with two little girls, my two older sisters. Showing them their baby brother.

Years pass by and William grows into a boy, an English boy in an Afrikaans school and the kids don't take to this kindly. The day was warm, pleasantly so as to still enjoy the host of outdoor activities and general adolescent camaraderie. Most kids have left school already. Having walked home or fetched by their parents. Such was not the case for poor William, who stayed behind accosted by bullies. That age-old schoolyard practice of verbal and physical jibes towards the meek, the "twerp" of the yard.

One of the boys shoves him to the ground, he lays there staring up at them. *"Gaan jy opstaan, Soutie?"* (Are you going to stand up, English man?) asks the one boy. They were playing with a ragdoll, picking the limp body up with taunting looks and greasy grins over their sweat stained faces, dropping him back down to the ground before he could find his feet. Shoe tips collide with his body as they mercilessly kick the air from his lungs. The pack mentality is always to corner and overwhelm the weakest buck. The irony was he knew he was the latter.

A pair of girls stood not too far off and watched with a defeated and silent consent at his pummeling. He recognizes one of the girls from class, her face covered in freckles and her hair in a ponytail. He wants to ask her to go get help but there is no air in his lungs to form the words. The chanting grows louder and William more scared, a boy steps forward and spits on him. Bleeding and sore, fear running through his body, without meaning to, he wets himself. The humiliation is at its worst, the crowd erupts into laughter at this. *"Jou pisgat."* (You coward) shouts a boy as he kicks him and his vision goes black. Their scornful jeers go silent and soon everyone leaves.

He lies there alone in his blood and piss soaked school shorts. The only sound around him were the sun beetles, not even the wind could be heard. He has blacked out and seems lifeless to anyone passing by. After a while he finally wakes up and pulls himself to his shaky feet. Bullying comes with its fair share of mental anguish too. Ego takes as much a beating as the body. His mind was racing with thoughts. Tormenting himself, cursing his weakness and failure to stand his ground against his opponents. Silent screams creeping from the black matter of his brain.

He picks up his school bag and a little red car, his favorite toy, and walks away thankful it wasn't taken. He wonders why he has to go to an Afrikaans school, the kids loved to pick on him and use him as a ball in their games. Life was painful and humiliating in school. Walking home, he feels so alone and doesn't know how to tell his parents about what happened.

He walks through the door and first thing he notices is the littering of beer cans along the floor, he is used to this site. He knows not to point it out, his father is home early or didn't even bother to go to work. He makes as little noise as possible, trying to disappear before his father can see the state of him, tip-toeing over the minefield of beer cans. His father was slouched down on the old tattered couch, playing his gentle tunes on the saxophone. He is dressed as usual, his work clothes of blue overalls covered in dirt; grime and paint splatters. There is a penny whistle next to him on the couch. William lived to listen to his father play, it was calming. It never lasted long, the storm always hit. A joint lying in an ashtray, burn-ing away as a half beer can stood next to it. He misses a step and kicks a beer can causing his father to look up. Paul smiles warmly and beckons him over, even in his beaten up state.

William shyly walks over, the closer he gets the faster everything hits him and he start crying. *"Whoa now, what happened to you? Was touch rugby a little rough?"* asks Paul. William saw concern on his father's face. His father gets a smell of him and leans away. Smiling lightly as he realizes what happened. *"They hit me father, and laughed, it was the older boys."* cries William. Paul gently lays down his saxo-phone and stands up, he picks him up. *"Come now, my boy. Why, you crying? This ain't no funeral melody. Don't let those boys break you like this, you know you are my little warrior."* answers Paul trying to encourage his broken-down son. He shakes his head in disbelief. *"Show me those muscles."* asks Paul. William refuses. *"Come now."* says Paul more seriously. He shyly shows his muscles. Paul puts him down. *"Now you listen to your father, one day there ain't going to be no one to keep back my champ. You hear me! Come now, let's get you cleaned up before the real boss comes home."* states Paul leading his son to the bathroom.

Time has a way of looping it seemed, and small victories were often followed by hard falls. Paul is lying on the couch, it's later in the day and sports are buzzing on the television. He is lying on the floor playing with his red toy car. Through the window, he sees his mother approaching. He excitedly gets up and runs to greet her and help her carry the groceries. She opens the door and smells the air, sees the beer cans and angrily drops the bags. He picks up a can of rolling peas. She looks down at him. *"Sorry my child, take it to the kitchen for mom please."* asks Merissa.

He puts all the cans in the bag and carries a few in hand. Some hanging by a finger turning red from the tip of the nail down to the base of the digit. He ignores it, wanting to help out. Paul half dozing is now awake, he switches the television off and starts cleaning the mess. *"Long day, I assume."* says Paul. She nods her head and sighs, she walks closer. Merissa sees the half smoked joint still lit and suddenly anger consumes her. *"Paul Austen, jou rubbish!"* (You trash) shouts Merissa. Paul stands up, trying to calm the situation. *"My love, it's not what you think it is. I can..."* starts Paul. *"You think I can't smell it?"* interrupts Merissa. Paul throws the dagga joint into an empty beer can. Merissa is disappointed more than anything. *"You promised me that you won't."* she cries. Paul tries to comfortingly put his arm around her, she pulls away.

William walks back into the room. *"Look, your boy got his first battle scars today."* replies Paul trying to change the subject. *"And you are proud?"* states Merissa. *"Stop being so uptight, you have got food on the table. A roof over your head, what more do you want? Stop faffing my darling, you know everything will be okay."* answers Paul. *"Okay! Okay! I slave at two jobs all day and you?"* screams Merissa. *"I fixed Suzie's car."* replies Paul. William is watching this with fear, he knows what is coming, he sees the disgust in his mother's face and waits for the fallout. *"I should have listened to my mother."* says Merissa walking past Paul. Angered by her statement, Paul grabs her and accidently rips open her blouse.

Samantha, William's sister, hears the familiar sounds of a fight and comes running into the room. *"Daddy, please don't. Please Daddy."* begs Samantha. She runs to stop her father but he pushes her away, the force throwing her to the floor. William sits on the floor with his knees drawn up and his hands over his ears as the shouting escalates. But he can hear every foul word, every one piercing to the soul. He hears his mother scream as she is hit down by his father.

Anger and a sense of protection boils over and William gets up and runs to the kitchen. He searches the drawers 'til he finds a long and big knife. He climbs onto a chair and starts to hit away at the power box. Paul sees this from the corner of his eye and drops Merissa and runs to William. *"That's dangerous my boy."* says Paul trying to get to the knife. He turns to face his father, knife still in hand. *"Give me that."* yells Paul. When he does nothing, he pleads with his son. He drops the knife and Paul picks it up and places it out of reach. Paul looks at his frightened family. He turns and walks out of the house without a word of apology.

He waits until his father is gone, then he gets off the chair and runs to help his mother who is lying on the floor crying. A red mark forming from Paul's hand. He places a caring hand on his mother, she pulls away and stares past him at Paul getting into the car and driving away. He looked around, he knew his father wasn't always a monster. He was mostly in a really good mood, especially when he was stoned. He would play his sax and sing. However, if you wanted to really hear him, you only needed to follow him to Sophia town and watch him jam the night away.

CHAPTER 2

Sophia Town

Growing up in one part of a vast young country can be very different from growing up in another, and in South Africa this difference is not only a matter of geography. The division of the people into two great races; black and white. And the subdivision of the white into Afrikaans, and English-speaking groups provide a diversity of cultural heritage that can make two South African children seem almost as strange to each other as if they had come from different countries. My father would escape this world when he would sneak out late nights into Sophia Town, to play penny whistle with other musicians. The soulful melodies would fill the space, it was an escape to Patrick, from a world divided, a world of failing and surviving. Here he with other musicians made others dance, they were the heroes of the night. We only heard the murmurs from other people in town.

He told me it was a place like no other, a place where a man can be whatever he wants to be, whether good or bad. Here you can meet your brother from another mother. A place where you can find an American barber shop standing next to an African herbalist store with its dried roots and dust laden animal hides hanging in the window. Where you enter a small shop and made to feel big. It was a world much different than our own, a free space filled with all kinds of people, admiration and emulation of American culture, Shebeens, flamboyant American style gangsters (Tsotsis) with chrome-laden American cars who spoke a slang called Tsotsitaal and constantly played music.

All I knew it was a world much unlike our own, as my father described it: It was a fast-paced place where you pay your ten cents and get whatever concoction is there. Rich and poor, all were gathered together for the music and to dance a dance called the phata phata (touch touch). It started from Friday night right through to Sunday. If the police came during a drinking session, a signal would be given by the look-out. Bottles would be hidden, a painted veil of sobriety hung and new reason found for the gathering; a meeting with a minute book and matters arising always worked well. It was often that the police came for spot checks, and on this particular night they came with the intention of finding him. The police had an informant, someone telling them what was happening in and around there. My father still took the chance, believed it was worth it. On that night, however as they got into the place, he quickly ran to the bathroom and pushed himself through the narrow window, getting out before the raiding began. Paul covered his head with a hat and started walking down the street, seemingly unnoticed.

He had a skip in his step as he walked down the corridor in the house and entered my room. We all knew he went out every night, but no one said anything, especially in front of mom. He walked up to me and gently stroked my face, I would always smile at the presence of his gentler side. He gestures to be silent with a finger to his lips and walks out of the room and to his own. He knew we were told never to speak of this fantasy world. Mother always said: "Daar is genoeg skandes." (there are enough scandals already) But secrets always came out, no matter what.

It was early Sunday morning and everyone was getting ready for church, the birds are singing and the family have their own traditions. My father was up and eating breakfast, ready for any odd job he can find. My mother was also in a good mood and I stood on one leg. My sister and brother and I played this game to see who can last the longest. My one sister had gone to a friend for the day. Jason is my younger brother but he brings light into my life and fun after the bullying from school. Jason falls over first and I cringe in pain but stand my ground. About to fall, we heard a loud commotion outside. Mother walks over to the window, I follow her and see crowds forming on the lawn.

Mother covers her bruised face with her hair as there is a knock on the door. She goes and opens it. *"Morning Officer."* She says. *"We will just be a moment, we need to take your husband in."* replies the first officer. Mother got worried. She looks behind her at all of us watching. *"I don't want to press charges, just go."* she pleads. *"We are not here about your house disturbances. He has stepped over the line in more than one way."* answers the second officer. The police don't wait for a response, they enter the house and grab dad. Twisting his arms behind his back. *"Jy dink jy kan speel met ons?"* (You think you can play games with us) states the first officer. *"On what charges do you burst into my house on a Sunday of all days?"* shouted my father. The officers smile and cuff him roughly. *"I can smell them on you, you color blind?*

Don't you know your place?" whispers the second officer yanking him towards the door. *"My children, my dog? I have no idea what you are talking about. Do you have papers for this?"* he spits out. They ignore him and haul him outside towards the van. Neighbors looked on in silent disgust as my father was hauled away towards the police van. People he had shared a meal with once, now silently judging. The more my father struggled, the more the cops beat him.

William stands by his mother, suddenly running to his father's rescue. William hits an officer in the face and leans over his father's body to protect him. The police officer looks down at William disgusted. *"Ontspan klein mannetjie"* (Relax little man) says the officer lifting his baton. Merissa runs towards the chaos. Shouting as she goes. *"He is just a little boy, please understand. It is his father."* Paul, now bleeding, is trying to stand up. *"I am not a little boy."* Shouts William standing in front of his father. The officer smirks down at William whilst the other officer throws Paul into the back of the van. His family has gathered now to watch, tears run down Merissa's cheeks as she falls to her knees. The door is shut and Paul mouths *'I am sorry'* through the bars. The van pulls away and the crowd disperses, William tries to run after the van but his mother holds him back.

It is interesting what one sees in the dark, what lurks in the shadows. For a young child whose father was taken away abruptly, it can bring with it unimaginable fear. This was exactly what little William was experiencing at night. Everyone was asleep, apart from him lying in his bed thinking of his father. He pulls his feet up onto the bed, nothing touching the floor. A loud scream escapes but no one hears. The sounds coming from outside his room are like children crying in agony. With the last of his bravery he jumps off the bed and runs out of the room. The passage is filled with half lit, dark, dwarf like figurines. They grab onto his pajamas as he runs along, fighting for freedom. Calling out silently, terror caught his tongue so that no one could hear his cries.

He makes it to the room and jumps onto the bed, hiding under the blankets, shaking and scared. His sudden movements cause the cat to jump up and wake Merissa up. *"William!"* says Merissa still half asleep. She turns and sees the fear in this small boy of hers and takes him in her arms. *"What is wrong, my boy?"* asks Merissa rubbing a hand down his shaking back. He points to the doorway, not a word said. His sister walks into the room, awaken by him and is not

kind to her brother for waking her up. *"He saw something again, this time probably the Boogieman."* answers his sister. They get out of the bed, William being pulled reluctantly by Merissa, she leads him to the dark doorway and shows him the silent and empty passageway. He holds onto her leg, looking for anything amiss.
"You see, nothing there. Now go to sleep, please."

Darkness has a way of finding you when you are broken, brittle and scared. Waiting to attack, waiting to hold onto you. I was a young boy, missing my father and not understanding the world. Waiting for the next bullying, waiting for something bad to happen. I had no idea where to find him, and I couldn't speak to my mother about it. We kept moving to avoid him finding us, my mother was scared, rightfully so. She had enough on her plate trying to keep the family going.

It is a sunny day and he is on a mission, he is in his old neighborhood looking for his father. His mother is working late and won't know he is missing. He looks around, so much is still the same yet completely different. The cars have changed, the girlfriends have too. But the gossip and struggles in life was still the same for everyone around there. He sees a familiar face, an old man in a wheel-chair. With a small greeting, he walks on by. His suitcase and photo in hand, looking all over for the man he calls father. He asks a few people, many saying they haven't seen him in months and others trying to gossip as he walks away. At first it hurt, this was his father they were talking about.

Later it became like a cloud, merely passing by. As he turns to walk away, a bus drives by, coming back from the mines. Paul is sitting inside after a long difficult day of being underground. Suddenly he notices William, jumping up and running to the front of the bus. *"Stop the bus."* screams Paul. *"Sir this is not a stopping spot, please sit down."* answers the driver. *"Please sir."* pleads Paul giving a firm squeeze of the driver's shoulder. The driver relents and stops the bus, Paul jumps off and looks down the street. A few meters away is his boy, standing there forlorn. *"William. William!"* calls Paul. He looks up and at that moment it was like time standing still. Both staring at each other, before breaking into a run. *"Look at you, you are no longer a little warrior. You are growing so quickly."* He smiles at this, excited for the praise. Paul looks at his son for a long, seemingly endless moment. *"You still remember the game arcade?"* asks Paul. He nods and together they walk off towards it. They played for a few house, enjoying each other's company. He received from his father a whole bag of chappies (gum). They went to sit by a dam, chewing some. Paul opens one and reads the small printed fact. *"Did you know that in the US, Halloween is the second highest grossing commer-cial holiday after Christmas."* reads Paul. William shakes his head and looks down at his own chappie paper and read out loud. *"Did you know that your brain is the size of your two fists put together."* says William. He puts his two fists together and frowns. *"Really?"* sighs William. Paul smiles. *"You are still growing my boy."* He smiles, he knows this can't last. It is getting late and his mother will begin to worry.

The sun is setting and Merissa arrives home. She finds Jason and the other kids but no sign of William or his school bag. She walks around the house, calling his name. Merissa walks up to Jason and asks him if he has seen him. He shakes his head. Worried, she heads towards the window, it is getting dark fast. Suddenly a car approaches, an oh so familiar car. Merissa pours herself a glass of wine to calm her nerves. William gets out of the car along with his father, Merissa downs the glass of wine and walks outside. She feels mixed emotions at seeing Paul again. Merissa takes him harshly by the arms and starts pulling him towards the house.

Paul reaches out and tries to talk to her. *"How could you William Austen, you never do that again?!"* shouts Merissa. *"But mom, I…"* starts William. He is interrupted by his mother once again. Paul is following behind, trying to get a word in. Paul comes closer and she turns to face him. *"If you ever come near my child again."* yells Merissa. Paul looks down at him then her. *"Our child."* answers Paul. *"You stay away from us, you hear me? If you want what is good for him, then let him be."* says Merissa tears rolling down her cheeks. *"He came looking for me, true's bob. Found him walking around our old neighborhood. I did not take him."* answers Paul. Merissa looks down at William who nods shyly.

Merissa walks William to the door and ushers him inside. *"Can't we negotiate, maybe I can come around once every two weeks? Or I am willing to help pay. Come on I know you need me… or well he does."* asks Paul. It was the same voice he always used to get his own way, it always worked on her before. Merissa looks at Paul, standing right in front of her. He places his hand on her arm. He looks through the window, hoping this means he gets his family back together. *"You had your chance to be a father and husband."* replies Merissa. Merissa turns away but Paul is still holding her arm, Merissa pulls free forcefully. *"Get away from here or I will phone the police."* she threatens. Paul looks at her pleadingly. *"Please Merissa."* Merissa walks straight into the house and to the phone.

Paul knows this means trouble, he doesn't have a clean record. He gets in his car and drives away, exhaust fumes filling the air. William, Jason and his sisters watching from the window. He clutches the chappies tightly, these were from his father. His mother approaches, hatred in her eyes for the man she was once married to. *"William, you will never do that again."* scolds Merissa. *"I am sorry mom, I want-ed to…"* starts William but he is cut off by his mother grabbing him and dragging him to the room. His brother and sisters watching quietly. He loses grip of the chappies and it scatters to the floor, he cries out but still his mother drags him to the room. Through the closed door came sounds of the beating of his young life. His siblings still in the same spot hear his cries and watch wordless out the window. After that, the splintered family moved. The first time, but not the last. In some insane way, it was the only way to avoid their father. To lose him, forever.

William Austen

CHAPTER 3

We started over, a new life, new beginning. Mom wanted to be close to us, so she left her old job and started one at the boarding school we were enrolled in. She did every job possible, from ironing clothing or working in the kitchen. She cleaned hallways, all to give us security after in the absence of our father. Early mornings we stood in lines according to age, there were strict rules to follow. The bathrooms were more like temples for bullies, away from prying eyes. We were close to our mom yet it felt like we were worlds apart, we were still treated differently in the school. Not being with my brother was difficult, at home we were there for each other. That wasn't the case at school.

It was all very confusing, I was away from my father and brother and sisters. Even though my mom was there, a rift had developed. As is the standard practice in Dorm houses, we were split by gender. The only time we actually saw each other was in the food hall. In a strange way, my time here prepared me for things to come, by not having those I love close to me. It never occurs to people the similarities between boarding school and the army, or prison for that fact. The rigidness, walking in lines, reciting hymns in an unenthusiastic chorus. We'd have a set time for recreation, then it was back to the cells. This was the place I realized I would not see my father again, and something in me broke.

I created a version of myself where I would be seen as strong, hard-edged, so I joined those that were in control. One particular night I remember. I took to being a part of a group, the way you make friends by way of satiating attention through mischief. I think back now as a grown man, and I wasn't really a model student as a teenager. We took our bed linen to an empty room, way past midnight which meant we were caught, we'd be in Big trouble. Setting the linens on fire, like the lost boys of Hermanus making campfire in the dormitory. This made me feel like I belonged, it made me feel tough. More importantly it made me feel like I was part of something. It wasn't long before others ran to the room to stop the fire.

The next morning we went to class, it wasn't long before I was called to the principal's office. In the office, my mother was already waiting there with a look of disappointment in her eyes, I would see this look many more times in my life, mostly with tears following suite, crying for me, crying for help, just crying. I wanted to comfort her, to speak but no words came out. I sat down next to mother, the principle looked at me sternly. His lash lying on the table, my naughtiness would come at a price I would definitely feel. His strong hands beat down on my backside, I tried to be brave, to be strong. This was the punishment we endured back in those days. Knowing the others would have their turn afterwards. After that I went to lunch, it was the usual peanut butter sandwiches spread so thinly it might as well be nothing at all. While the daily kids had a lunch, box filled with all kinds of interesting and wonderful things. I probably shouldn't have complained, I had a roof over my head and food, well at least that is what mother used to say.

It wasn't long before my mother and father got divorced. We once again packed our things and moved on from this boarding school. We packed what little we had in boxes, which was little to say the least. Having moved so many times you learn to own a little and pack light. Financially we always struggled, we moved to the plots in Ermelo to start fresh. The standard practice was that we'd only move to get away from my father.

Life was hard to say the least, we as children understood very little but the reality we were growing up in. We called this place Gaggapark. Often, we stole potatoes from nearby farmers, most of them straight from the ground. Some weren't ready yet, but mother cooked them anyways. This was the life we were living, soon our family found a friend in Merissa who moved in with her children. She had also run from an abusive husband, they spoke about it in private at times, the two women, but it always ended in tears. They tried to be strong for the children, it was their own strange way of protecting everyone.

Me and my older sister Lolla were worried about the financial struggles of our mother, so together out of our heads we came up with a plan. We gathered all the clothing we could find and then put price tags on it. Using white sticky paper and markers, we made reasonable prices for our young minds could conjure. After that we went to the street and as workers walked to and from work we tried to sell to them. At first, they looked at us strangely but soon a crowd began to form. The bag of silver grew till it was about full and we were filled with excitement. We wanted to show our mother what we had done. Merissa was home late, as she was many evenings. We jumped up, forgetting how tired we really were, excitement overtaking. *"Calm down."* said Merissa. We led her to the kitchen and showed her the bag of money. She looked at it curiously but with a calm shocked after thought. *"And this?"* asks Merissa. Lolla told her the story, Merissa's face turning into all different emotions from anger to anguish. Merissa ran to her room, seeing all the hangers on the floor and the few pieces of clothing left in the cupboard. We had only tried to do good, Merissa kept her anger in check. Merissa walked back to the kitchen, she looked at the money and said nothing. We never got into trouble or anything. Merissa knew this was something special, maybe even sacred in a way.

I loved my mother, she was broken, yet strong at the same time. Merissa got us a few Doberman dogs to keep us safe. Jason had a dog named Power, he was the strongest of them. Fast, yet loving. During my growth, I spent a lot of time with them, they were a sense of hope to me. They grew up so fast, yet one didn't last long. One cold evening everything changed, the farmer we rented the plot from had sheep grazing on the other side of the fence. He was a strange old man that kept to himself mostly. One night, his sheep were attacked and killed by a wild animal, he thought it was our dog Power. We never knew what type of man he was till then, we heard our dog bark then give a cry like never before. Me and my brother Jason ran from where we were playing to go find Power. The farmer stood with a "windbuks" (Air Rifle) and was shooting at Power. He shot the dog numerous times, seemingly taking pleasure in his act of revenge. We were crying and screaming over the sound of the gun firing for him to stop. The dog was bleeding and yelping, and the farmer just kept reloading and shooting again. He shot him in the ears and mouth, even putting the gun against his chest and firing. Through all this Power never tried to run, he stood his ground and tried to protect us from this man. The old man shot the dog in the face and he finally fell down, his breathing laboured and slowed.

I ran to the almost lifeless body of the dog; his suffering had felt like forever. For a young boy like myself and my brother, we carried his body back to the house, the old man staring us down. A hate boiled inside of me, a catalyst for things to come later in life. Wanting to shoot this man the same way he shot our beloved dog. What kind of man, no better yet creature would do something like this? We tried to cover his bleeding holes and make them stop, praying and calling for our mother. He took his last breath in our arms, it was a sad moment for us all. We buried him under his favourite tree and decided living here was not possible anymore.

After moving again, it was time for me to start high school. This was a scary notion for many children, but I already knew what was going to happen to me. As we entered the premises the Grade 12's were in charge and made it known. We were told to put our suitcases on our heads. It didn't stop there, we were called fungi and told to put plastic bags on our heads to stop the rot from spreading. This was a common ritual, we called it "ontgroening" (initiation), the grade 12's figured they earned it from surviving it themselves all those years ago. Whilst the teachers were telling us how to get acquainted and showing us around, the grade 12's were showing us fear and power with their hierarchy. We were not to look at them when they spoke to us and careful to answer their questions.

Break time was filled with all kinds of activities, from having to wash their cars to measuring a girls' legs from the shoes up, using a matchstick. This was nerve wracking for both parties. The older boys would laugh at our nervousness, yelling at us to go faster. If the match dropped, you had to start over again. At one stage, during lunchtime, I walked into the boy's bathroom to find a group of older boys lifting the grade eights into one cubical. The cubical was bursting at the seams, boys crying out at having no space. They were Like animals. I turned to walk away, but they spotted me and grabbed at my collar. I was lifted up over the sealed door and into the over-piled cubicle. There was nowhere to move, hardly any space to breathe. They were probably trying to break a record or something and we were the game.

Suddenly a male teacher shouted for the door to be opened, it was yanked open so fast we all fell to the floor on top of each other. The older boys tried to keep their composure, acting like there was nothing wrong. They weren't really good at acting. *"What do you think you're doing?"* shouts the man, red faced in his ugly brown woolen suit. *"Nothing, sir."* The boys shaking their head. We all shakily got up, dazed and taking deep breaths. *"Go wait for me in my office."* says the man. The older boys just laughed and walked away. *"The rest of you, clean yourselves up. If you tell your parents you will have me to deal with."* He walks out of the bathroom. As usual I kept my mouth shut and headed out.

One of the various school rituals for grade eights was to have a school concert.

Whilst rehearsing behind the curtain, I waited for my turn. The same group of Afrikaans boys walked up to me, by now I know them well enough for the way they treated me. The play was in English, to my benefit, and I was given the lead role for my strong English background. *"Is jy al ooit gebliksem, soutie?"* (You ever been punched, Englishman?) questions Danie. I step back, the boys check if there are any teachers around. *"Ek soek nie moelikheid nie."* (I don't want trouble.) I said in my slight English-Afrikaans accent. *"Moelikheid?"* taunts Danie. He looks back at the other boys and smiles before smashing his fist into my nose. I fell to the floor as blood gushed from my nose, the boys laughed and walked away. Everything was fading to black as pain radiated throughout my body.

    I watched them run off as a teacher yells at me for causing trouble again before leaving me there. The last thing I saw was my younger brother's face, everything went black. I woke up a while later, dry blood around and on me, my brother just sitting crossed legged next to me. It was late in the day and school was already out, no one had come to help. Usually Jason was the only one to help. He went as far as getting himself beat up just to protect me at times. Together we were a team.

CHAPTER 4

The two boys walked home together, blood staining William's clothing. His nose swollen and purple. They approached the plots and the first person they saw was their mother's new husband Richard. He was a priest, a Holyman, cut from the cloth. They barely took notice of the man, but he made their mother happy. He and Richard had a mutual dislike for each other. He saw this impostor as a shallow replacement for his absent father. Richard was working on the old Volkswagon, smoothing out the body with fine sandpaper. Richard stopped and watched the boys approach, their mother stepped outside with a cold drink for Richard. She noticed William's face and concern flashed on her face.

"Wat het gebeur my kind?" (What happened, my child?)asks Merissa. Merissa places down the tray and touches William's face, he pulls away from her. *"Let me go, please."* replies William, embarrassed. Richard put down the sandpaper and faced them. He liked to call them Stiefseuns, acting as though they were a functioning family unit. *"Stiefseun, jou Snopkop! Jy praat nie so met jou ma nie."* (Stepson, you lit-tle brat! You don't speak to your mother like that.) shouts Richard. William looked at Richard with clear defiance. *"Jy is nie my pa nie, jou gryskop aap."* (You are not my father, you grey-haired ape.) says William angrily. *"Ek slat jou oor hierdie blerrie kar, hoor jy?"* (I will knock you over this damn car, you hear me?) screams Richard.

Things were escalating fast between the two, Jason bumped William's shoulder to get his attention away from Richard. They walked to the house, avoiding a more heated altercation. Richard loved to point out that they weren't his children. To him they were the Devils of the old, an old life that was wished away. A man no one thought deserved to be a father. Richard had strict rules and that were to be obeyed at all times, the Bible read nightly.

Christmas was a big occasion for the whole family. Merissa would bring down a tree and decorations, sometimes the kids made their own. It was a rare occasion where everyone was happy. They didn't have much but they were in good company. Merissa cooked a large meal, the meat cooking in the oven with gravy and all sorts of vegetables on the side. Richard wore a father Christmas suit to impress the kids, but Jason and William just thought it was funny how his stomach was pressed tightly in his shirt. *"Ho, Ho, Ho and Merry Christmas."* bellowed Richard in a deep voice, hiding his face behind a cheap white fluffy beard and small oval shaped glasses. Merissa was impressed, Jason made fun of Richard as he turned his back. William and Jason laughed at their own antics but stopped as Richard turned to face them. It was an impromptu pantomime performance on the boys' part. *"And this one is for William."* says Richard handing William a small box. *"Wait, let me guess, hmm, a watch."* sighs William under his breath. *"If you manage to keep this one and not break it, we won't need to buy you another one."* replies Merissa. He shows Jason the watch. *"We might even be on time for church for once."* giggles William. *"He looks like a baboon's ass."* responds Jason looking at Richard. *"No, like elephant shit."* laughs William.

Richard ignores the boys and hands presents out to the girls. Merissa puts down her cooking utensils, calling Richard over with her eyes. *"We have some news."* says Merissa. She walks up to Richard who takes his beard and glasses off and wraps his arms around her waist. *"We are expecting a little one."* states Merissa looking at the boys. The boys looked at each other while the girls excitedly ran over to Merissa, hugging her and touching her stomach. *"What do you think William, A boy or girl?"* asks Merissa. He looks at Richard then at Merissa. *"A boy."* he replies. Richard glares at William. Lolla oblivious to the tension, twirls her hair and smiles. *"No, it is going to be a pretty girl like me."*

It was a family ritual to go to the Vaaldam. Merissa was very pregnant and showing prominently. She was calmer and so was the family life, everyone helping to make things easier for her. All attention went into her and the pregnancy, even Richard seemed to not be so uptight with the boys. William helped his mother out of the car, she waddled over towards where the girls were setting up the picnic blanket and basket. Jason was already stripping his clothing off and running towards the water. *"Last one in is a rotten egg."* yells Jason running full speed towards the water. William smiles and heads to the water, the heat of the summer accompanied by a cool breeze.

Richard has set up six rods by himself, he took his fishing very seriously. He had given up on trying to get the boys interested a while ago and now did it by himself. Richard looked over at the boys splashing in the water and then at Merissa sitting in the sun. *"William, Jason come put up the tent for your mother."* calls Richard. William lets go of Jason that he had been holding under water and starts walking out of the water. Jason follows behind, trying to catch his brother. William was always a little faster.

Once the tent was up, everyone went about their own business again, Richard had a net in the water to keep the fish fresh he caught and the boys were back in the water. At the end of the weekend, the fish was placed on the top of the car in a bag. So on the way home, it becomes difficult for Merissa to handle the smell of the fish and the sound of them flopping around and dying on the roof. When they stopped somewhere, Richard walked off and Merissa looked at the two boys feeling gravely ill. *"William, please."* asks Merissa. William and Jason got out of the car and found a spot to dump the fish, placing the full bag with luggage back on top of the car. The boys giggle between themselves and get back into the car.

Richard doesn't seem to notice a difference, playing Christian music loudly in the car. They stop along the way further to eat small sausages and eggs around a picnic table. William and Jason play games in the car to entertain themselves. Everyone got out at home and stretched their legs, Merissa and the girls went inside. Richard takes the fish case off and opens it to find everything but fish in it. He angrily looks at William. Richard's face turns red with anger and he points a finger. William and Jason run towards the house, Merissa comes out at the loud commotion. *"Genoeg is genoeg, en jy beter teen die tyd al jou plek ken stiefseun."* (Enough is enough and you should know your place by now boy.) shouts Richard. Merissa approaches Richard and lays a calming hand on his arm. *"Richard please, it was me. I told them I couldn't handle the smell and the sound of them dying."* cries Merissa. Richard yells at Merissa, she sends the boys inside. William goes to look out the window. Expecting Richard to raise a hand to his mother. Instead they stood outside talking until it grew dark and wandered inside silently.

Revenge wasn't far off for the boys from Richard's side. He did it the only way he knew how. It was nearly time for school and that meant haircuts. Richard took the boys to a local barber with an old man who would cut their hair. They sat down and one by one their hair was washed. The old man started with William, scissors in hand. *"What can we do for you today?"* asks the man. Before William could answer Richard stepped forward. *"Ek soek dit netjies end kort."* (I want it short) replies

Richard. *"Please don't, the kids at school will laugh at us."* pleads William. *"Snot man, my familie gaan nie lyk so skollies nie. Nie eers my stiefseuns nie, hoor jy?"* (Nonsense, my family will not look like hooligans, especially my stepsons, you hear me.) scolds Richard. William hung his head, defeated, the scissors snipping away.

When school started it was back to normal, the bullies were back in action and William was terrorized daily along with Jason. He and Jason were getting big-ger and stronger, yet they still couldn't outmatch the older boys. They were outcasts, fighting to survive. William was frustrated with the way things were going. One day after school, William and Jason were walking home along their usual route. The normal biker gang sat outside their house and for once it drew his attention, they were the type of people your mother would warn you about. To stay away from them at all costs.

One specific person caught his attention, he was covered in tattoos and was punching a punching bag near the end of the garage. He was mesmerized by the power in his moves. He was fearless, the speed was remarkable that he moves at. There were coke bottles hanging from the roof with water in it, this was a strange place to be. He started walking towards him, Jason tries to pull him back. He shrugs him off and continues forward. Four other bikers sat at a metal table smoking weed and drinking beer, one has a gun on his side, he walks closer and the guy boxing stops and looks straight at him.

"You lost Chomma?" asks the tattooed guy. His name was Pieter. He was sweat-ing and breathing hard. The other bikers looked at the boy smirking, one tattoo stands out on Pieter. "GREAT HERO'S DEMAND GREAT OPPONENTS." Pi-eter looks irritated, he just shakes his head. *"Wat kan ek doen vir jou?"* (What can I do for you?) asks Pieter. He looks at his brother who looks scared and steps forwards. *"I want to fight like you do."* answers William. The other gang mem-bers stare at him in silence. Pieter walks past him and takes a bottle of alcohol from the table. Pieter takes a big gulp then faces him. "

Jy soek dit rof?" (You want it rough?) Pieter passes him the bottle of booze. Jason shakes his head but William ignores him and takes a big gulp. It goes straight through his belly and to his head. He tries not to react and keep a straight face. Pieter laughs and puts an arm around William's neck. *"Jy's oraait."* (You're okay.)

laughs Pieter. They offered William a whole new world, filled with drugs; alcohol and good old-fashioned violence. But he just wanted to know how to fight, he wanted to be good, he wanted the power and the moves. He wanted to stop fearing and start showing everyone who he really was.

That was a start to a new chapter in his life. He started training hard with them. Going home every day with a sore body and not enough energy to fight with Richard. He was venturing into a whole new world and Richard didn't approve. His days were spent at school dreaming about being back with the gang. Rich-ard tried to keep him in line, he forced the boys to go to church Sundays. They were biding their time until they were old enough to leave the house. William sneaked in most nights after being out late and this lead to him falling asleep often in class. Class was a waste of time. All he wanted to do was fight or practice fighting.

His first encounter would come sooner than expected, one night he and Jason went with Pieter and the gang to the grungy bar called the Pleasure Palace. There wasn't much there but pool tables, games and people escaping their boring life. They left drunk out of their mind, ladies on their arms. For William, this was fun and a great introduction to the real world. He wore his favorite Batman t-shirt with the sleeves torn off and watched Pieter play pool. Their rival gang was led by Braam. A man they all hated and stayed clear off. Fights between the gangs got heated but one or the other fled before it got to serious.

Tonight, of all nights the gangs were at their separate pool tables bumping each other to cause missed shots. He wanted in on the action, so when Braam was about to shoot the black ball in and win he bumped him so that he missed. By now his muscles were showing, even though he was still growing. He turned, pretended it was an accident but Braam didn't let it go. Braam was pissed and turned to face him. *"Jy soek vir Kak klein mannetjie."* (You're looking for shit little man.) growls Braam. William kept on walking, slowly past him. *"Jy doof?"* (You deaf?) questions Braam. That was the last straw, everyone was staring at him. The adrenaline pumping through his veins, something he could easily get addicted to. Braam's gang started walking towards him, he was outnumbered and slightly scared. This meant trouble.

One guy had a glass bottle held as a weapon, walking slowly. William turned

to the door to run, but was blocked off. Seeing an opening he ran for the stairs and made his way up. Fighting going on downstairs as he ran away. Feeling like a naughty boy running from a prank. But to his dismay, the door was locked at the end of the passage. The only thing available was a utility store room filled with cleaning supplies. He slid between boxes and hid himself, making himself as small as possible. William could hear them walking around, looking for the boy.
"Kom Batman, jy is mos braaf." (Come on Batman, you want to be brave.) Shouts one. They open the door and switch the light on, it flickers. In fear William holds his breath. They look around then leave. Releasing the breath he held, I wait for a while.

It must have been a few hours, by the time he went down the bar was empty. The victory was short lived, he made my way towards Pieter's house. Every-one sat outside with a beer, William's brother with a piece of meat over his swollen eye. The night was a small victory for him, his brother had taken one for him. They left and headed home, dreading what's to come. Slipping inside, their mother sat at the table in the kitchen. Jason snuck past before she could see him, but he was called forward. *"William my boy."* said Marissa. William stepped forward, reveal-ing that he was alright. *"All is good mom, no worries."* replies William. *"Jou pa is 'n priester en kyk hoe gaan jy aan. Die mense praat, skaam jou man."* (Your father is a priest and you behave like this, people are talking. Shame on you.) scolds Merissa. "Hy is nie my pa nie." (He is not my father.) grumbles William.

The noise they made woke Richard, he would be angry at the lateness of the night. Tomorrow was church and they always went as a family. *"Nou hoor jy my… More oggend wanneer ek kerk toe gaan. Gaan jy en jou broer saam. Jy het koor, hoor jy?"* (Now listen to me, tomorrow when I go to church, you and your brother will go with. You will be part of the choir.) shouts Richard. William shook his head, he did not want to be a part of this society of ill religious pretenders. Once Richard made it clear, he left the room. *"Asseblief William."* (Please William.) pleads Merissa. He could see the weariness in his mother's face. The baby was being weaned and she didn't get much sleep. He was exhausting but she loved the baby. It brought her and Richard closer together. They were a new family and William and his siblings were the products of a dark past, one Richard tried to keep in the past.

The sun rose early that Sunday morning. William could hear Richard getting ready and felt the need to just go back to sleep. But he knew not going would lead to more trouble. He and Jason stood outside the church smoking weed before everyone else came. He felt so out of place, Richard was respected here. They served him loyally, he was a Servant of the Lord. He and Jason were dressed in choir robes and stood in front of the church congregation. Richard treasured his people especially the German family, probably for the cheque they left at the end of each month. The congregation stood up to sing, he was irritated with a German boy looking at him in disgust. The boy turned to his friend and whispered, pointing and snickering at William.

He looked at this boy and he snapped, the boy acted as if he was superior to William. William grabbed him by the tie pulling it tight. The boy grasps for air, his arms flailing. He raises a fist but an elder man stops him. *"Hierdie is God se huis."* (This is Gods house.) says the man. Merissa puts her head in her hands hiding in shame. Richard steps forward as the whole church watches them. Richard shows for them to sit down, the tension still high. Richard ignores what just happened.
"Liewe broers en susters" (Dear brothers and sisters.) says Richard. *"Gesaamtelik is ons hier vergader in Sy naam, verhewe bo alles."* (We are gathered in His name, higher than all other names. continues Richard.). *"So lief soos God ones vader ons gehad het."* (God has loved us so much) states Richard.

William was furious that Richard didn't even address him, he threw his choir book forward, hitting the pulpit. A dead silence fills the place. Richard was furious but he kept it reigned as he looked at him. He stands up and walks to-wards the door. The old man who had pulled him off of the German boy stood up outraged. *"Hy kan nie mos so maak nie en dan uitloop nie. God is n God van orde."* (He can't do this and then just walk out. God is a God of order).

He turns to face everyone from the back of the church. He was waiting for anyone to do anything. He makes a gesture with his hands for anyone to challenge him. *"Nou man Asseblief. Dissiplineer my. Enige iemand, almal van julle."* (Then come, please and discipline me. Any of you, all of you.) Yells William. He stares Richard in the eyes defiantly. The church members all talk amongst each other, unsure what to do. No one dares do anything. He laughs at them. He walks out and slams the door shut behind him. Jason followed after him, they were both laughing and walking home. Together as usual. To them church meant belonging, meaning and hope, to William it meant wasting his time reading a book filled with rules. This was the last time he went to church. They returned home to find the garage door locked. He was still so angry and refused to stay locked out. He tried hitting it with a brick but it did nothing. His next option was to slightly open window of the garage. They forced it open and climbed inside. Once inside they turned the place upside down, destroying everything of Richard's. They searched the room until they found industrial strength glue and squeezed it into a bag and started sniffing it. *"I feel nothing."* Says William smiling. His eyes were showing the effect but he didn't care. Jason lifted a plank up and with a hard punch William snapped it into two. They continued doing this with a few more planks. Once the boys ran out of planks they entered the house and ran around like lunatics.

The domestic worker walked through the door with clothing in hand. She hears a noise then walks towards it surveying the mess. He slams a fist through the door right next to her head, she screams and he laughs. *"Jy moet nou stop met die gom. Daai goed gaan jou mal maak."* (You have to stop with this drug, it will make you crazy.) Shouts the woman. He puts his arm around her shoulder and hands her the bag, she drops it to the floor. He angrily shows her his fist. By this time church has ended and Richard and the family are driving home. Richard is livid not sure what awaits his return. The domestic worker runs out of the house, stopping the car. *"Hulle breek die huis my baas."* (They are destroying the house, sir.) Screams the domestic.

Richard walks into the house surveying the damage, glass all over and doors broke. He walks to the bedroom and hears laughter. Through the broken door he sees him and Jason jumping on the bed, they look at him and laugh louder. Richard is furious. He knew he couldn't stay in this house much longer. After they got chased out of the house, everyone else started to clean. He over the high walks through the fields around the house. He sees the postbox and walks towards it and gathers the mail. It is the usual, bills, letters from church members. But then one letter stands out, addressed to his mother from the military. He runs back to the house, Richard is picking up his broken things and gives him a disgusted look. Richard can't stand the sight of him, so he leaves the room.

William shows Merissa the letter, she is shocked, knowing what this means but never imagining the time would come. They opened it together and it stated William was being called to military training and service. Merissa looks concerned at her first born boy. *"You can still finish school."* Says Merissa. He shakes his head, this is his way out. *"I can write a letter, you just need to tell them you want to finish school first."* sobs Merissa. He looked at his mother seeing the same image from when his father had a rage session and knew he had to go, he was no good for them. He didn't know how to tell her he needed this. He wanted to please her but him staying was just destroying her. She was adamant she wanted him not to go, but this was for the country, this was a way out. She gave him a hug, holding tightly, he felt like a small boy once again who loved her hugs and tears welled in his eyes. This was his ticket out of here but he was leaving behind his best friend and a mother that loved him no matter how badly he acted out. No more school, no more church and to be honest the thought of holding a gun excited him, one legally and with the right to kill.

The Angolan War had started just after Angola was declared free from Portugal. This led to a civil war in Angola, this however was to be considered ground zero. The ground for the Cold War. Heavy integration of the Soviet Union and United States made this their playground. Rich in resources, Angola was politically and economically devastated and would see the land stained by the blood of young men sent to fight a war far from home.

He stood in his room packing his bag. Jason entered the room, more quiet than usual. They both looked around the room that had become their home and sat quietly embracing each other's presence. They were best friends and William's life would be hard without him, what would he do, how would Jason cope? They had endured so much together and were always there for each other. Now they would be apart and a small part of him wasn't sure if he would return as he had left.

A big crowd of family members and town members from far and wide, all coming to say goodbye. The men proud and the mothers scared, the fathers thinking my boy will bring joy to our name. The soldiers marched in and the young boys were led away as the song is played "FIGHTING SOLDIERS FROM THE SKY, THESE ARE THE MEN OF THE GREEN BERET."

William marched with the others, Jason and Merissa crying as the train left. Not much was known of the war back home, not much shared in the media. South African government however found ways to grow the country economically as well as military wise without all the tension. The Soviet Union sent in large amounts of military hardware and trainers to the Angolan army FAPLA. Cuba also played key roles with forces of up to 55 000 in strength. With a total of almost 380 000 Cuban military personnel serving in the country from 1975 until 1991. If the SWAPO took over it would bring conflict right to the borders of South Africa, it was strategically important to eliminate the threat. This was going to be a whole new world for William and the other young men entering training.

William Austen 34

CHAPTER 5

Basic training included but wasn't limited to Pole PT, this was a two-man training session. One pole held on either side and the men running along it. The poles used to make marks on our shoulders from the rough terrain. We had to complete a specific distance in limited time. Excessive PT was a popular form of punishment. When inspection days rolled over we had to be clean shaven; our fingernails clipped down to the pink, shoes shined and our beds had to be immaculate. Failure to meet these standards meant your ass in a sling. The biggest, brutish men cried the loudest. These sessions could last upwards of four hours.

We could hear our Drill Sergeant yell and spit fiery insults in the thickest Afrikaans voice: *"Hardloop! Stop! Draai om! Stop! Op jou Maag Meneer, kruip soos 'n wurm! Spring so hoog soos jy kan! Push-ups! Noem jy dit 'n Push-up?! Doen sommer vyftig meer! Stop! Drink water. Doen dit weer!"* (Run! Stop! Turn! Stop! On your gut, crawl like a worm! Jump as high as you can! Push-ups! You call that a push-up?! I want fifty more from you! Stop! Drink Water. Now do it all again!) By the end of it you'd be lucky to walk away. We'd vomit until all that was left in our stomachs was bitter water. When we started, we were soft, putty ready to be moulded. As time went on, we'd be carved from stone. What seemed like punishment in the beginning became routine. We'd all be in tune with one another. We'd run farther; jump higher and every push-up we'd force the earth down. If one person failed, we all failed. We had to be ready. Your brother beside you an extension of your arm. This was done not for self-satisfaction, but for commitment to our country. It was war after all.

I loved the sound of bullets firing, the feel of the rifle jerking against my shoulder. The power it carried, the power to kill. I hated the Afrikaans Corporals, who made sure everyone knew I was English. I hated the discipline but learning to shoot was something I looked forward to. Firing an R4 was one of the greatest experiences of my life. Learning from the best on how to shoot. How to breathe and keep the gun steady. Every time I hit the target, I felt a sense of pride swell in me. I became proficient in handling the weapon. It was like learning to walk. Being a good shot would earn you a badge of excellence.

Most of us were still kids in the eyes of the people, 16 and 17 year old boys being handed guns and told: *"Vir volk en vaderland"* (For the Motherland). We would walk a full 10km march with our gear. A rat pack, gun, extra boots, knife and fork. Once you start walking up and down the hills the gear felt like it would get heavier with every step taken. This would easily take more than a day. We had to work sparingly with our resources. The food and water had to last us the full duration of the march. Graduation day came close, which meant we could see our families. We stood on a rugby field in formation. Clean shaven and in perfectly pressed uniforms, with our General standing before us. After three months, we had the opportunity to go home for a week before the second phase would start. When the opportunity came to volunteer, I hastily took it. The Corporal entered the room and asked who would volunteer, myself and two other guys put our hands up. That was it, the start of action. Little did we know of this new journey, soon we left the base and headed out to a place known as Olifantshoek.

We were the crucial link to the men on the border. All correspondence came through the signal men from five signal regiments who were operating on the mountain. We were assigned as guards, signal regiment. As a joke we built a coffin, and wrote a letter on its lid: *"Hiermee begrawe ons menslikheid."* (Herewith we bury our humanity). We stayed in small rooms, right next to the gate of the mountain. We were armed with R1 rifles. We took shifts patrolling the gate, always keeping accounts of who came and went. Always keeping a watchful eye. But we had to find a way to keep ourselves sane. We broke many rules while we stayed there. We were in charge and decided who could come up. It was a power play that we enjoyed.

William and Du Toit walked around, patrolling the mountain side, it was the early night shift. It was quiet, no one moving but them. Suddenly something moved, without thought William turned and shot without second thought. Only to realize afterwards it was a "Dassie" (A small rodent indigenous to Southern Africa. Known as a Rock Hyrax or Rock Badger). We were given rounds to shoot out for the day on the mountains as a way of keeping our aim sharp and our minds at ease. Another incident took place, I recall, we were watching rugby and drinking heavily. When our team lost, we looked for a way to vent, so we went outside and fired as many shots as we could up into the mountain side.

Before we knew it, we got called from the signal regiment and asked what the commotion was about. We lied and responded by saying we saw opposing military men, APPLA. And were shooting at them. A huge investigation took place. "Voetsnyers" (Trackers) came to our base and searched for the men to no avail. In the end, we had to own up to our lies after the empty bottles and bullet casings were found. We were reprimanded but we still hadn't learnt our lesson, on another occasion we ran naked through the streets. There were thirty of us running drunk and naked, finally caught by the police and brought back to base. But the last straw was us going into a bar drunk and causing fights, walking home most nights beaten and bloodied.

My time at the war was coming to an end, the many antics we did were causing them trouble. We had painted an elephant statue pink and our final act was one for the books. The new troops were being moved to Olifantshoek, Ferreira and I knew the new troops were spooked coming out here and we decided to scare them. It was time for a proper welcoming. Du Toit helped them prepare for this one, he climbed the dish which was 25 meters high. He had a dummy stuffed with tomatoes in military overalls with him. He pretended to sit with Ferreira but was actually alone with the dummy.

I stood below with the troops signing in, and looked up. *"Du Toit moenie dit doen nie, asseblief"* (Don't do it, please) I yelled. *"Ek kan nie dit hanteer nie, ek is moeg vir die lewe."* (I can't handle it anymore, I'm tired of living) cries Du Toit from below hidden away. Ferreira tries to stop him, but then pushes the dummy. Everyone watched in horror as the dummy fell to the ground with a hard thud. Red tomatoes splattered everywhere painting a scene with faux gore. These were good times. I was one of the lucky few to have come back with such stories. Most would come back in coffins.

Returning home was not easy, settling in with my family after being away was harder. I returned to my two sisters already out of the house and back to being called "stiefseun" again. There was no big ceremony, no special meal. I returned to a setting I had run from in the first place. I tried to avoid all contact with my stepfather, but it was difficult. Richard and my mother had been divorced twice since I had left, but seemed to always get back together. My mother was in the church a lot and her youngest kept her busy.

Everyone minded their own business and kept to themselves. Jason and I were back together as a team, a pair of misfits getting up to endless mischief. Getting drunk and breaking into houses for the fun of it. Being chased through the streets and looking for fights. Smoking and drinking and just taking over the area. Jason had two big German shepherds and we would drive through town with Jason's car with the windows rolled down. Jason was driving illegally but no one seemed to do anything. We loved to scare the townspeople by riding past and commanding the dogs to bark loudly. Those who didn't run away would scream vulgar obscenities at us. Even church people I recognized from what seemed like long ago.

I came back as a man filled with pride, yet having only finished 9th Grade there wasn't much for me in the working world. I couldn't go back to school. So, I started looking for whatever place that would hire a high school dropout. This would give me an income and a break from the home atmosphere. It didn't take long for me to get a job though, a toyshop had an opening as a sales person. The toyshop was by the mall, opposite a bait and tackle dealership. I saved everything I could, and eventually I bought my first car. A Mazda 323. It was not that bad a job, smoking weed and being able to test out the latest toys. I had learnt the toys off by heart. I took pride in helping people find just the right toy.

Some days I stacked the little soldiers and re-enact what happened overseas. A happy boy walked in with his shorts one size too small, jingling with coins. He took one of the toy soldiers and placed it down with his money. I knew it wasn't enough, the boy was slightly disheartened. So, I smiled and wrapped the soldier for him, telling him to not tell anyone. The boy left the store with a skip in his step and a large smile on his face. I watched as the boy took his soldier out, pretending to shoot it. At the end of the day I counted the money and took what was needed out of my allowance. I would lock up and stop by the local shop on my way home.

I was barely eighteen and in my eyes, I was a man. The first thing I noticed was the new girl working behind the counter. She was tall but still shorter than I was, with blonde hair that fell over her shoulders like an angels' halo. She had big doe-like brown eyes and this shyness that seemed to radiate from her. I was captured by her beauty, and up to the task of asking her out. She looked to be sixteen, younger than me, but I didn't much care. I walked up to the counter, confident as ever. *"Chesterfields please."* I asked. She looked up at me and handed me my cigarettes.

I payed for it and walked out, as I lit a cigarette I felt the need to look back at her. She smiled at me. Little did I know how much I would fall for this girl. My world was about to be turned upside down. I had nothing to lose.

CHAPTER 6

The sun had risen on the cold winter morning and William was up early and at the shop cleaning out. He had already packed the toys neatly but time was dragging on. Today his manager was in and busy going through the books. William dreaded how quiet it was when the children were all back to school, his thoughts lingered on the pretty girl at the local shop. He wanted to work up the courage to talk to her, and not just ask for cigarettes. The manager was busy counting up stock as William quietly approached him. *"Sir, is there any way I can take my lunch early today, while it is quiet please."* asks William.

The manager was quiet, calculating a sum in his head. He just nodded in reply, not acknowledging his presence. *"It's all quiet 'til about one sir, I came in early and aligned all the stock. My mother needs medicine because she isn't doing well at all."* William lies. The manager put down his pencil and looked at him. *"Alright, but you better be back before two. You know how busy it gets after school hours."* Answered the manager. He hurriedly went to the back to take off his work shirt and put on a clean blue one, one of his best. He was really excited about seeing this girl.

As he arrived at the shop he could see the girl working behind the counter packing the shelves, adjusting his collar he walks in and strides towards the girl, confident in what to say. Until he got to the counter. *"A pack of Chesterfields please."* He asks. *"R3,50 please."* Answers the girl. *"What is your name?"* William asks, fighting back the urge to break out in a nervous sweat. The girl looks over her shoulder at him. *"Are you new around here?"* She asks. *"Oh no, just came back from the army."* He says proudly, not taking his eyes off her as she hands him the cigarettes and takes his money.

As he walks out he realizes he still doesn't know her name. He waits for a moment, turning to walk back in, but stops and proceeds back to work. He walks into chaos; the schools ended early and the store was packed with over-energized children waiting to pay for their toys. He rushes to the back, putting on his previous shirt and running back out to help the manager with the sales. He gets things under control before the manager completely loses it. For a moment,

Wiliam thinks back to his childhood playing with Jason for a moment. The simpler days he had.

After work he decided to take a different route home. He hope there would be a chance of seeing the girl again. The fact of the matter was he still didn't know her name. The sun was hallway set on the horizon and the street lights slowly came on as William crossed over the road and around the corner to where the shop was where she worked. By a stroke of luck, she was still there. She'd finished her nightly duties and was on her way to locking up. He waited. He felt shy about the idea of walking up to her abruptly and asking her name. That small voice nag-ging at the back of his mind: *"What if I scare her away?"*. What felt like a lifetime came to an end when the girl finally locks up. He had made his presence known earlier by way of a sheepish wave. He never felt the need to scale back his personality before. He felt a real connection to the girl. A childish notion of feeling infatuated.

As she secures the large steel gate, he pulls from his bag a small plush toy dog from his bag and hands it to the girl. *"For me?"* she asks, taking the toy from William. He nods. *"To keep you safe."* He answers back. The girl smiles at William with a kind of warm intrigue, a silent invitation to walk with her. To keep her company. The sunlight softens on the horizon in shades of warm oranges and indigo light, slowly turning colder shades with each passing minute. The distant clang on the headlights as scores of moths butt heads enthusiastically with the fluorescent bulbs. He walks with the girl. A short silence broken by the utterance of a name: *"Mandy."*. Her name suited her perfectly. It rings and bounces off the walls of his mind. He smiles the dopey kind of smile like a toddler seeing a puppy for the first time. To say he was smitten would underscore his feeling giddiness at hearing her name. He mutters her name excitedly to himself. The chemistry was palpable between the two with such an intense degree.

Mandy stayed in what was known to the general public as a "Blikkies Dorp" (Tin Town- Colloquial slang for the poorer residential areas) Most families had one basic income to support everyone. And most of it would be spent on booze. Her stepfather was a violent; alcoholic chauvinist who regularly beat her mother to the point her face would look stitched on; bright purple and red. The years of abuse had turned her into a cold, shell of a woman. Broken and compliant. No shred of joy would cross her face. The house Mandy stayed in was overcrowded to say the least. The stench of cat pee and dog faeces over the musky scent of unwashed carpets and stained, broken couches wafted over in sickly green hues when you stepped through the door.

The homely environment of the no-collar community. The Miners-House. The decorations ranged from old china figurines placed on a dusty mantle underneath paintings of some obscure landscape with rivers and forests to rusty; broken down cars on the front lawn with sickly grass slowly creeping up the sides. The appeal of such an environment was akin to cancerous lesions. Many of the people in the area came from good familial standing at some point or held stable jobs. But the economic situation and dooming end of apartheid had caused a lot of changes. The misuse of drugs and alcohol became the chief concern amongst the jaded community.

Mandy's stepfather lived on disability pension, living off the backs of others while drinking his woes away. William feared he would lift a hand to Mandy. He grew to hate the man with a passion. Mandy never felt comfortable when they went to her house and tried to avoid it as much as possible. Most of their night were spent lying on the hood of William's car; listening to music and getting to know each other. For the most part this kept William out of trouble. Fromm time to time he would spring cash from the register at work and spoil Mandy. But William felt he owed her a real date.

Life at home was a different story for William. Late nights with Mandy caused a rift between him and his mother. Harsh words would be tossed around freely by his mother, broken by yet another divorce from Richard and his little brother occupying most of her free time. Even though she looked tired and worn, a glimmer of beauty still shined from her. *"What's her name?"* William's mother asks. *"Mandy"* he answers sheepishly. The time was close to midnight and his mother was up and waiting for him to come home. Before further words could be said, he knew what his mother was thinking. She scolds him for foregoing his education, which he abandoned when he joined the army.

After that night, he stopped seeking approval from his mother for his pursuit of Mandy. She would not see eye to eye with him on the union. When morning broke the next day, he arrived at his work a little after his usual clock-in time. The manager stood at the counter with the books, fury painting his expression. He knew what was to come before it came. What seemed like the longest time in William's life was over in minutes as the manager screamed obscenities at the young man. He knew he would eventually be caught for stealing money from the register, and so prepared himself for the inevitable encounter between him and the manager. No warnings were given. In fact, the manger wasn't granted the chance to complete the resignation practice as he turned halfway through his tirade and left.

The next evening he was at the arcade. He spent a lot of time there waiting for Mandy to finish her shift. *"Have you ever been to the desert Mandy?"* Asks William. *"No."* she answers. He takes her hand and walks down the arcade isle with her. The night was young and the arcade was packed with people. Mandy looked up at the stars, joined by him. *"They say you can see the stars more clearly in the desert."* Mandy says to William. *"I can take you, if you want. Jason and I are planning to go to Namibia, to go past Zwartkop, to have a good time. I would love it if you could go with us Mandy."* William says excitedly. Mandy pulls away, hugging the bear tight. *"He won't let me."* she replies. *"Your stepfather?"* he asks. *"I'll speak to him."* he continues. Mandy shakes her head and steps back. *"You don't understand William, it's not that simple."* replies Mandy. She sobs as he pulls her closer. *"I love you. He won't touch you."* He pulls her closer and kisses her passionately.

Early in the morning Mandy walked down the dank streets of her neighborhood towards her house. She could hear the sounds of the TV blaring loudly from the cracked windows and indiscernible; drunken yelling. Most nights her mother would be out; helping in soup kitchens or attending prayer group. Any excuse was a valid one to get away from the drunken ramblings of her so-called husband. Mandy hesitates going in. She knows what her stepfather was like at night. She takes the chance. Maybe he won't notice. Through the lit curtains, she sees him go to the bedroom and takes the chance.

She rushes to the bathroom and locks the door behind her. She listens for his heavy footsteps through the door. Mandy looks at the stained cast-iron bath-tub and proceeds to undress. She lets the shower flow, feeling the cold water turn warm in her hand. She turns to look at the locked door for a moment, then at the small heap of clothing. The little bit she owned herself as she stepped into the shower. The door buckles and breaks as her drunken stepfather bursts through the door, his bloodshot eyes looking Mandy up and down like some rabid beast. The TV blares loudly over the screams in the bathroom. Anyone who heard didn't care enough to do anything. The stars hidden by thick gray clouds.

It was past midnight and William was sitting on his bed, smoking his last joint for the night. He hears a soft knock on his window and he gets up to look outside. He sees Mandy standing there, shaking in the cold. Immediately he opens up and helps her in, she falls into his arms. He saw something was wrong, she was covered in bruises. *"Take me to the desert. Please William."* She pleads. *"Who did this?"* William asked. *"Please just take me away from here."* Sobs Mandy. William nods, holding her tight. *"We'll make a plan. You'll come with me to Namibia."* Answers William.

The streets glimmered with shards of broken bottles. Thin, gray clouds slowly moved on as sunshine crept through, shining on children playing barefoot in the streets. She was sleeping in her bed. A soft knock was heard on her window, waking Mandy from the lightest sleep she's ever had. William stood in her yard, looking straight into her bedroom. Hesitation takes over for a second as she looks into the living room at the passed out drunken heap of her stepfather on the couch. In a fleeting moment, she tosses a small bag of clothing at William and climbs through her window. They run towards a car parked outside their rusted gate with Jason at the wheel and get into the back seat. *"Welcome, lovebirds."* Jason jokes as William holds Mandy tight. They pull away from her house with fury as William kisses her on the forehead.

CHAPTER 7

The sun crept past midday, not a single cloud was in sight. The long winding road heading northbound had been traveled for nearly 9 hours and the trio was feeling tired and hungry. Grassy fields dotted with the odd set of trees surrounding on each side. *"Time to stretch our legs"* William says looking in the rearview mirror at Jason and Mandy, half asleep. The car stops just a few feet from a thorn tree, the ground blanketed in green grass. William and Mandy walk towards the shade of the tree, Jason followed close behind with a small picnic basket and blanket over his arm. The gentle breeze rocked the leaves back and forth with the three sitting just at the edge of the shade, passing around sandwiches. Not another soul was in sight.

The remaining path to the Namibian border became difficult. The tension was palpable the closer their car came to the border gate. One always felt nervous entering a new country. The usual questions were bouncing around: *"What if we're turned away?"*; *"What if they arrest us?"*. The paranoia hung thick as she realized she didn't have the proper documents. William kept a calm demeanor. *"Relax, babe. It's been sorted. I made a few arrangements before we left."* Answers William. As the car pulled towards the gate, patrolled by men in heavy gear and automatic weapons, he became nervous. A layer of sweat glossed his face. He handed the stern-faced man the collection of papers and for a moment the wait seemed never ending. He walked towards the booth, discussing the papers with his colleague. After an eon of waiting, he is handed his documents with "Approved" stamped over all three's papers.

When the gate opened, William had fought his best self not to speed away into the distance. Once the gate was clear from sight, the trio hollered in joy. Their troubles were left on the other side of the line. William lights a joint on their way towards "Swakopmund", a coastal city with its roots in German colonialism. She hangs a small crucifix adhered with stones around the rear view mirror, a silent symbol of her escape from her beastly stepfather. The sun hung low over the surreal plateau of Namibia. The wind carried the salty smell of the ocean as their car neared the coast.

The next day as Mandy and William walked along the beach they came across a seagull on the sand, flapping about wildly leaving patches of blood behind as it moved. As they stepped closer the bird began moving less. It was dying, and Mandy was in a state. When he kneeled down to the bird, it seemed quiet and eventually, faded into stillness.

Out of everything that "Swakopmund" had to offer, the beach was the place they spent most of their time. They rented out a bungalow and called it home. Their haven. The slot machines kept them busy, and from time to time got lucky. The carefree drifters lifestyle. Drinking; eating and watching the sunsets. Mandy meant a lot to him. His first love, his everything. What really knitted them together was the trust between them and being far away from all their woe. They felt inseparable. Days spent recovering from the night before, never leaving each other's side. Regardless of it all, he and Mandy had no place to go. They would escape into the desert dunes. Blasting music; drinking hard liquor and making love under the night sky.

One evening Mandy and he went back to the bungalow earlier, Jason stayed behind a while longer on the beach, knowing well enough it wasn't because William was tired. The two young lovers walk up the wooden steps of their bungalow's front porch. He holds her by the waist and leads into the bedroom in a conga line kind of way. She giggles at this behavior. They were starry eyed, but they had long since become sober. He places Mandy on the bed, and they undress each other, between each kiss an item of clothing falls to the floor. They make the love the old way. Tenderly kissing each other all over between every stroke. Their most fragile moments together.

That next Friday, as they left a bar, he walked out with heavy steps with a half full bottle of liquor. Mandy and Jason were walking behind him in uncharacteristically quiet moods. Blood was slowly drying in patches across William's shirt. *"We were just playing rough babe."* William slurs, looking at Mandy. She starts walking faster, storming past him. Jason takes a step back when William runs a short distance to catch up to Mandy, dropping his bottle. Jason kicks the bottle under a car, and out of sight. They were arguing. Earlier that night he got into a fight, and in his drunken state beat a man bloody. Harsh words are thrown back and forth between him and Mandy. Some nights he enjoyed the occasional "one drink too many", and she didn't like the way he acted in this state. What would normally be associated with the term: Blackout Drunk. The argument became heat-ed to the point Mandy started crying. Beating at his chest. He grabs her hand and pulls her close. Holding her tight as she sobs.

The time rolled by and soon their getaway came to a screeching halt. Money was low, and his growing habits became frequent. Somewhere down the road the car begins making an ungodly noise, and black smoke started gushing from the vents on the hood of the car. They pull over in the middle of nowhere and not an emergency telephone box was in sight. Under the hood was a smoking mess. The car had some distance on it and was in need of a service. Most cars passed without hesitance until a man stopped his Jeep behind them. The man was a local. Dressed in a canvas buttoned shirt and the shortest pair of khaki's a man of his portly frame should never be seen in. His work boots were dusty and scuffed from repeated exposure to the dry Namibian elements.

He strolled closer to where William was standing, his hands tucked in his pockets as he takes each awkward step. *"Iets fout?"* (Something wrong?) he asked. His breath was heavy with the smell of brandy. *"Lyk my die gasket het geblaas Oom."* (Looks like a blown gasket, sir) William sighs. The man peaks under the hood half-heartedly. *"Nee, seun. Hierdie kar gaan nerens heen nie."* (Nope. This car isn't going anywhere soon). The man takes out a handkerchief and blows his bright red nose, wiping away the snot. *"Sal Oom ons kan help trek na die naaste dorp toe?"* (Would it be possible to tow us to the nearest town?) William looks at the man.

He contemplates the request in silence for a moment. *"Jammer jong man. Ek gaan nie nou naestenby 'n dorp verby nie. Ek is juis op pad huis toe nou."* (Sorry young man. I'm not going anywhere near a town now. On my way home actually). After an awkward pause, the older man walks towards his vehicle, *"Hoop jy kom reg, meneer. Ek wens ek kon help maar het nie eens 'n tou om die sleep nie."* (Hope you get sorted. Wish I could help but I don't even have a rope to tow you).

He drives away, leaving the three in the middle of nowhere. William looks as he drives away: *"Ou bliksem."* (Old Bastard). Time crawls by and the sun sets down low over the horizon. William; Jason and Mandy have taken to playing cards as every car passes without looking out their windows. The sky turns from blue to a warm orange, if there were street lights they'd have come on by now. *"So, I assume we're sleeping in the car tonight?"* Mandy asks, looking at William with a slight look of scorn. *"This isn't my ideal scenario. We'd have passed Upington by now if this heap didn't break down on us."* He looks back at Mandy with wounded pride.

The headlights of a car shine through the rear windshield onto the mess of cards on the backseat. An old BMW with Gauteng license plates. An older couple gets out and walks towards the car, William gets out and reasserts himself. *"Naand. Het julle dalk help nodig?"* (Evening. Do you need help?) the man asks with a kind voice. *"Asseblief Oom. Ons sit langs die pad al heeldag lank. Daar's fout met die engine."* (Please, sir. We've been stuck on the side of the road all day. The engine stalled) William answers. A few hours later, the three found themselves on the more familiar side of the border. With whatever money was left William paid to get the car mobile again. Driving through the Northern Cape towards home what seemed like a never-ending drive.

Mandy was lying on top of Williams chest, fast asleep. Everyone was exhausted after months in Namibia and the long drive back. A loud knocking at the front door wakes everyone in the house. He gets up to look out the window, expect-ing the police, but sees her stepfather. He picks up a cricket bat and storms down their hallway past his now awake mother. His bat had more to say than he did. As soon as he yanked the door open, an intense screaming match commenced between the two men.

Her stepfather was drunk, his face sweaty and his nose red from the hard liquor. In most cases, the wise decision was not to fight with a drunkard. Her stepfather had looked deep into the bottle that day and was flipping through emotions like a light switch. Sobbing and yelling like an impatient child, demanding his daughter come home and wailing through snot and tears for her to go see her mother. Through his bedroom window, she was watching. Eventually her stepfather left, tripping over his own steps towards his car. He spun his tires and drove away in a fit. William stood at the door until he couldn't see the car anymore.

It didn't take much time before they would once again find a way back into the humdrum of routine. William found a better job. Since his mother threw him and Mandy out, he needed to be able to afford a place for them both. For a while they had to live in his car. Every few months they'd move back in with his mother when she had time to herself. But the pleasantries were short lived and soon William and Mandy were back on their own. Kicked out again. This became a common practice. After a few months William began to settle into his new job and started earning well. Whilst he kept a good profile at work, the mischief didn't stop. And after more than a decade, neither did the desire to find his father. For years he hasn't seen him and no clue where to even start.

On one special occasion, they had an awards evening. A fancy conference hall packed with people, snacks and wine served as they talk. Various business men and women walk around, people slowly starting to find their places at decorated tables, the staff from the fine furniture company was attending the millionaires grow awards. This was pure boredom to him. He looks over at Mandy in her elegant evening dress. If she hadn't come along; the evening would have been torture. The others in attendance became boisterous with every passing hour. Bragging about their past achievements. Awards for various achievements were handed out.

Although a formal event, it felt like a school function to William. He looked at the stage where his CEO was handing out trophies. The CEO looks into the crowd and looks straight at William. *"The next award goes to William Austen."* Says the CEO. Mandy gives William a kiss on the cheek before he stands up, and walks towards the stage. This is the first ever award William has gotten. *"You my boy, have a bright future in this company."* The CEO said to William, shaking his hand. The rest of the evening William danced with Mandy.

The repetitive corporate lifestyle started to unsettle him. It was boring to him. It lacked the excitement he craved in his army days. To cope with his stress, William began to drink more. He was looking for any way out. Any way to numb his settlement. And one day it came crashing into him.

CHAPTER 8

The shop was particularly busy, He has set up a karaoke system at the shop and is illustrating to customers how it works. With snacks on the side, the young men were surely interested in buying. William being good at targeting the right people to sell to. During lunch time, he was called to the manager's office. *"Austen, I need to give you a warning. This is not about you, but I was told that we are going to have to let staff go. Bad three months and head office isn't happy, we will only be able to keep a few of our best sales agents if we don't reach target again."* It was an annual practice. The threat of losing his job, even in good months. It was their way of keeping the employees on their toes. It just helped them increased profit.

William nods as he walked out back onto the shop floor. Later, William was standing outside in the heat smoking a cigarette to calm his nerves. He notices a red Holden Minarro driving towards the shop. He always had an interest in cars. He used to sit outside and watch them drive by as his father and him played cards. William walks in front of the car in absent minded amazement. The driver slams the brakes to avoid hitting him. *"Are you crazy!"* Screams the driver. He walks to the driver's window still in a trance. "How much for the car?" Asks William. The man laughs. *"You want to buy my car. With what money?"*. He looks the man straight in the eye. The man laughs and looks at his girl next to him. *"Elf Duisend rand."* (Eleven Thousand Rand) says the man jokingly. William nods his head. *"Eleven thousand, come and get me here at 5, right here, you got me."* Replies William and walks back to the store. The driver with a puzzled look on his face drives away.

William, back at work, felt more like an auctioneer than sales consultant as people flooded in. Running one bargain to the next, people stock their trolleys with various potential household clutter. A man stops outside the shop with a truck, he calls towards William. The manager can see William talking to the man and shakes the man's hand. The trucker sends in men and they start carrying out stock, a lot of stock. The manager walks to him after the man has left. *"William what is going on? A sale this time of the month?"* Ask the manager. *"We got to keep making our tar-gets sir, don't want to be back out there now do we sir."* Questions him.

"You know we have to check with head office before we do such a discounted sale William." Scolds the manager. He looks at him angrily. *"First you say we have to reach target, now you want me to stop selling."* Replies William. *"No that is not what I mean."* Sighs the manager.

He is unsure how to handle the whole situation. He takes his name tag off and places it in the managers hand. *"I'm sure you will find someone very willing and young to be your next favorite sales agent of the month."* He turns and walks out of the shop with his money in hand. As the sun was setting, the Minarro drives into the parking area. He walks up to him and takes an envelope filled with notes out from his back pocket. The man starts counting the notes after William gives it to him.

The man climbs out of the car and looks at it. For a moment, he stands next to him not saying a word. The last bit of sun was shining down over the town as the man hands the keys to William. *"Thought you were joking, trying to impress my girl."* Laughs the man. *"Why did you come back here, you like her?"* Questions William. *"The ride, all comes at a price and you made a good one."* Answers the man, the man gives him his keys. *"Take care of her."* The man walks towards the bus stop. William excitedly gets into the car and drives home to show Mandy and Jason his new pride and joy. Mandy sees him through the window and runs towards him. *"Where did you get this?"* Asks Mandy kissing him. *"I bought this for us baby."* Answers William.

He was kissing and undressing her, a few empty liquor bottles were lying around on the floor. He gently strokes down Mandy's naked body with a gun in the other hand, that he puts down next to the bed. He passes her a joint that he is smoking. She smiles but rejects the offer. *"It is going to be okay."* says William kissing her again. After thinking for a while, he knew it was time to move on, Mandy and himself had to go on the run. What he had done at work to make the money for his car was wrong and he was sure the police would be called. The next morning the car was packed and he was in a hurry. His mindset was that whoever stood in the way had to take a bullet. Anyone who tried to separate him from her would face this mad man, his life was Mandy's. It was the most dangerous place to be. There in not a person more dangerous than a man crazy in love. When they ran low on fuel from being on the run, they'd steal it.

Fill up at the closest petrol station and drive off.

The duo decided on robbing people, a fast way to get money. The person would usually give the card and pin without a fight. Not wanting to die for pieces of plastic. They were told to give the code for their account, otherwise they would come back to finish the job. It was months of this, Mandy was good at seeing the easy targets and William enforced the threat. They made a good team, one of trust and passion. They were feeling full of power, he loved the fear in their eyes when he held any type of weapon and threatened someone's life. It was pure victory, walking away knowing you would be taking what was theirs. They lived in hotels, ordering room service and enjoying the luxuries. Using the jacuzzi and living the high life. By morning they put the do not disturb sign on the door and would slip out the window without paying. Get into the Minarro, all their stuff still packed. They would drive out of town and let the v8 roar, laughing as they moved on. Crime was their way of life. Their wild lifestyle reflecting Bonnie & Clyde.

One particular night, he parked the car a block away from a seemingly quiet shop. He observed what was going on for a while. He climbs out of the car, and puts the gun under his shirt. There were no CCTV camera's in sight. He walked to the garage he had been observing, followed an attendant to the pay point and took out the gun. *"Kom ons hou dit eenfoudig."* (Let's keep this simple) whis-pers William. He was becoming adept at this practice. The man was frightened, his whole body shaking as he got down on his stomach. He shook the gun at him. Taking the cash out of the till, making sure no one was coming. *"If I see you move!"* Yells William. The man was crying in fear, William walked toward him and placed the gun against his temple, loading the gun. *"Meneer seblief, ek smeek."* (Sir, please. I beg you) pleads the man. He loved when they begged, he was in charge and their life was in his hands.

Back at home, Jason had been working at the same furniture store. During supper at home a police car arrived. Merissa saw the blue flashing lights and walked to the door, unsure what to do. Jason walks past her and opens the door. *"Evening. How can we help you?"* Asks Jason. They were trying to look past Jason, but he kept the door mostly closed so they couldn't see inside. *"I think it's best if we sit down and talk."* States one of the officers. Jason had kept a clean record after he'd returned from Namibia. They entered the house and sat down with Jason and Merissa.

The house was silent, besides the sound of the Piet kettle whistling. Merissa left and returned with cups of tea into the lounge. Her hands were shaking as she brought it in. Jason took it from her and the officers to help themselves.

"*The charges are very serious, if you know your brother's whereabouts, you better speak up now*" Says one of the officers. Jason sips his tea and decides to act dumb. "*What charges?*" asks Jason. "*For now, robbery, fraud, assault and kidnapping.*" Answers the officer. The second officer follows. "*We know he is armed and travelling in a Holden Minarro. A warrant for his arrest has been faxed to all police stations in the country. It is only a matter of time.*" They all sit in silence soaking up the news. "*I need you as the mother to understand. This situation is serious and can get out of hand. Your son could be killed.*" Merissa looks away, tears rolling down her cheeks. They turn to face Jason again, leaving Merissa to weep silently. "*If he gives himself in now, he might have a chance.*" The officers tell Jason as they leave.

William and Mandy were in a hotel, frantically packing their bags. The bed was littered with money, spread over the sheets and guns and underwear. After a brief phone call with Jason earlier, he was bone white with fear. "*We need to sell the Minarro!*" Mandy says to him. "*Grab what you can carry. We're gonna lay low for a while.*" he says in a panicked tone as he stuffs all the money he can into a suitcase. As per usual, their escape route involved the window.

I knew we couldn't run forever but I had to try, we had no destination really. We walked and hiked through the night. Exhaustion creeping in as daylight was seen. We hitched rides from one location to the next, sometimes I felt paranoid and wanted to pull my gun and scare the person driving us. But Mandy stopped me and we went on our way. This time as we were dropped off, Mandy stopped and looked at me. "*I won't go any further with you.*" says Mandy. This hit me hard. Normally our fights don't last long and we end up having sex afterwards. This time I know it was different, she has made up her mind. She sat down on the dirty soil with her hands in her hair. I walk towards her and placed a hand on her shoulder. "*I will find a way to fix this.*" I tell her. "*Just promise me you won't hurt anymore people.*" begs Mandy. I look into the distance at cars approaching. "*Will you come with me if I promise?*" I ask. She nods her head and stands up. When the road became quiet again, I dug a hole and buried my gun there.

They knew the cops were looking for them, going past townships, only white were found doing this stretch of work. They were once again vulnerable, not knowing where was safe to be. They stayed off the main roads, still smoking weed and drinking to stay sane. Stealing from ATM's from unsuspecting people drawing money. They stayed close together, making sure no security cameras caught them or people close by. It was survival every day for them, getting cash for drugs and some basic food or whatever was needed. Mandy changed her hair color to black to change her look and William shaved off all his hair. It was a chase between small places to stay off the radar.

It was a dark, misty night in Port Nolloth. The town is situated near the Southern Richtersveld region, top of Namaqualand. Not a place where the police would really go to search for a criminal on the run. The town used to be a seaport catering to copper miners, seafarers, diamond divers and many others. Now there was not much to the town. Officer Visagie and a few others walk towards Port Nolloth Hotel. Visagie indicates for the police to go around the back. He walks into the hotel and finds the clerk waiting outside the bar. Visagie speaks to the man. William was still seated in the Hotel Bar. Lined up in front of him was a row of shooters. He lifts one to take a sip and sees the police in the bar mirror, they have drawn their guns and were fast approaching, any fast move would end badly for him. *"Hands in the air, do it now Austen"* Shouts Visagie.

He was not scared to fight but knew this was not the time to pick one. He walks straight to Visagie, staring him in the eyes. There was a darkness burning inside William. If he could just get them away from here, Mandy would be safe. *"No sudden movements, you're surrounded."* Says Visagie. His gun pointed at William, William slowly lifts his hands up in the air. Two cops cuff him from behind and lead him out of the bar. They are moving him through the reception area and he sees Mandy standing there in cuffs. Still in her sleepwear, her eyes red from crying. *"You let her go, you hear me. She is innocent, I met her on the side of the road and she has nothing to do with this!"* He screams.

CHAPTER 9

Mandy wasn't speaking to William. She sat quiet on the cold, concrete floor of her cell. Across the narrow hallway was William, staring at Mandy. *"Babe..."* He calls. She doesn't answer. Twice more, under hyperventilated breaths William calls to Mandy: *"Babe, I'll fix this."* His go-to mantra when shit hits the fan. His natural attraction to mischief had taken its toll on the young woman. They'd fallen into routine as he had feared would happen. But the path not chosen wouldn't have led to their eventual incarceration. And there, on the cold, dusty floors of the holding cells, sat the two young lovers. Livin' hard and fast inside gilded cages. It was only hours later that the anybody outside took notice of the two.

Visagie came in, called Mandy's name and led her cuffed down the hallways towards the front. Acting like an impounded mutt, he sprang to his feet, screaming demands at the steely constable. It wasn't minutes later when another officer repeated the procedure. Erratic but compliant, he was led towards the front of the station. As he passed through the plain white door he noticed his mother standing near the discharges desk. Her eyes red, puffy and dry through her respectable make-up. Mandy sat on a white plastic stool on the other side of the room. He expected Jason to bail him out; and for a moment imagined his father might be the one standing there. But his mother, he never thought would come down. Shame spilled across his face as his cuffs are removed. He didn't say a word the whole way home as he sat in the backseat, alone.

The bail was only a temporary freedom. He and Mandy were to remain with his mother until their appointed court date came to pass. Jason of course, was ecstatic that his brother was home. Always close-knit, he regales his brother with his adventures and wildly romanticized all he had done. It was like being told the plot of Bonnie & Clyde in minute detail. Mandy and William slowly came to speaking terms again. The same could not be said for his mother. The only time they spoke was during arguments.

After a few weeks of being caught in the clutter made the living situation unbearable for William. Penniless and unemployed, William would spend his days fighting with either his mother or Mandy. The only person he had contact with outside the house was his sister, Samantha. She had married and had two children with her husband Gerhard in Windhoek. The conversation went on long on the phone. Samantha felt pity and out of misplaced guilt told William to come across the border where she would shelter him.

The prospect immediately enticed him, his mind had already wandered across and was enjoying a beer, safe from all that would seek to harm him. Although this time he'd be crossing alone. Taking Mandy would spur on a manhunt for them both. Although it was difficult, William had to leave without her. Early the next morning he packed a light travelers bag with only two pairs of clothing and a toothbrush. Jason gave him enough cash to take a taxi all the way to Upington, from there, he had to walk. He told his mother nothing, and only had a brief moment to say goodbye to a teary-eyed Mandy. On his way through the darkened streets towards the closest taxi rank, he was once again on the run.

He had to play it safe crossing over to Namibia. It wasn't strictly speaking the legal route. He walked for two days toward Windhoek to his expectant sister. Water was low and he was completely exhausted. Mandy never left his thoughts, but they were more worried thoughts about the state of her safety. The endless, dusty road was completely silent, not a car in sight. Not an ounce of shade for him to hide from the relentless sun was seen. His water was low and his socks were drenched inside his heavy boots. Like Sisyphus, he pushed forward his bolder to the peak only see it roll back down the mountainside. To land himself in this position of repeating a doomed cycle. He was a criminal now, a fugitive on his way to hide from his misdeeds and leaving behind only burnt bridges. He became a nomad of the justice system, doomed to pick up and move on, never finding rest.

The first month at his sister's house was relatively quiet. He kept himself low key and never went out, spending his afternoons playing with his niece and nephew and drinking during the late nights. Even breaking contact with everyone save for Jason. He felt to embarrassed to speak to Mandy. With no income, he was basically a squatter in his sister's home, much to the chagrin to Gerhard. He was an extra mouth to feed, an inconvenience to the family stability. Not much happened for the next few weeks. But one day, William received news from his brother that

Mandy's charges were dropped. Placid Samantha offered to arrange for her to be brought to Windhoek, but Gerhard was hearing none of it. He lived under their roof rent free for nearly 3 months. *"Nee. Luister, ek het nou genoeg gehad. Jy moet jou kak uitsort by die huis en ophou wegkruip hier soos 'n lafaart! Gaan pak jou kak. Ek vat jou border toe in die oggend."* (Listen, I've had enough. You're going back and owning up to your shit and you're going to stop hiding away like a coward! Pak your shit. I'm taking you to the border in the morning). Gerhard was furious, red-faced. William pleaded at first, but finally relented. There was no winning this time.

The next day Gerhard and William were on their way. Roughly 13 kilome-ters from the border to South Africa Gerhard stops. *"Van hier af is jy op jou eie."* (From here, you're on your own). He says to a silent William. No goodbyes were exchanged and before he could blink, William watched as Gerhard spun away. The walk was shorter, but William took slow strides towards Upington again. He wasn't in any rush to get back home. Later that evening as he entered the small town, tired and hungry, William pulled out his last two rand coin and placed a phone call home. Jason answered. *"Can you come fetch me? I'm in Upington."* William says in a heavy tone.

Although he was back. He wasn't home. Mandy was attached to him like they were new lovers. For the first time in months, his mother spoke to him: *"Dear. You know what you have to do. It's not ideal but it has to be done. You have to go to the police station tomorrow and own up to what you did. You can't have this peering over your shoulders forever. Think about Mandy."*

He did, all the time. He was arrogant at first, but finally made the right decision and the next morning… walked into the police station and straight to the front desk. *"My name is William Austen. You've been looking for me."*

CHAPTER 10

The court proceedings didn't take long and soon enough, sentencing was handed down. The judge looks down at he sitting in his father's old suit. *"Mr. Austen. This court wasn't gathered here to decide on an innocent or guilty verdict. That fact was made clear before proceedings began. The fact that you acted with such blatant disregard for the law has put me in the position of deciding the length of your penalty, and I say without hesitance that you shall spend no less than seven years within our correctional facilities for your erratic and violent behavior. Before you leave Mr. Austen, I would like to say that I see you as an animal. A mad dog on its way to the pound where it belongs. May this time you spend within penitentiary help you see the error of your grievous acts. Bailiff, could you please escort Mr. Austen to his holding cell until such time that he be transported to corrections. This court is dismissed."*

Gob smacked, he looks behind him to the stunned expressions on his family's faces. His mother had her face buried in a silken hanky and Jason was hold-ing her hand. Mandy, of all, was most shocked. As William is cuffed and escorted towards the back rooms of the courthouse, he looks at Mandy: *"Seven Years isn't that long. I'll be out before you know it. I love you."* He looks at Jason and his weeping mother: *"Look after them, please. Promise me you will take care of her"* he said with desperation in his eyes, knowing he is about to let go of the one person that gives meaning to him, to a dark unknown world. Jason looks William in the eyes but does not respond. The police officer pulls William to come with, but William stands his ground making sure Jason gets the message. *"Promise me"* he shouts. Jason nods his head as William is led out of the courtroom. Not a proper goodbye was said by the lot.

The prison grounds, surrounded by towering electric fences, barred wire, armed guards, a place to those who have nothing left to loose and somehow a place where many come to gain a new respect marked by their numbered tattoos representing their rank and gang.

A prison van comes to a halt outside the prison. He looks through the small window of the armed vehicle seeing two officers walking to the back of the van to unlock the steel door. *"Spring gevangene"* (Get out), the guard shouts with his voice creating an echo throughout the back of the van. He exits the van, cuffs on his wrists. The second officer immediately stamps down his authority as he violently push William with the baton in the back directing him to the entrance of the prison. *"Soentoe Bandiet"* (That way you criminal!), the officer demands.

At the entrance of the prison. He notice the large steel doors, at least seven foot. Once a man comes in here, theres little chance of getting out by your own force. One of the guards knocks on the door with the baton. Another guard from inside opens the door. Almost hesitant to take that first step into a world he knows nothing of. William obeys, and enters left foot first. He is confused, unsure of what is to follow.

Prisoners are asked several cursory questions then told to strip to bare bottoms. He enters the processing room and the guard looks him up and down. *"Wat noem hulle jou?"* (what do they call you), the processing officer asks William. He remains silent, observing the environment. The guard takes Williams docket from the police officer and writes the information down. William is commanded to strip and is hosed with cold water before being commanded to put on his jumpsuit. He has one photo with him of himself and Mandy, that he hides from their sight throughout the procession.

He is taken through to the cells, a long passage awaits, prisoners staring as he walks. The guard calls out loudly and everyone walks to their cells.

"Folla folla folla", the guard shouts. The prisoners run and gets into a line, two in a row and squat. The guards count as they obey their commands. Another guard is walking behind counting the prisoners. They are being watched by other armed guards, further away behind the enclosed gates. The guards send the prisoners to their cells and the steel doors are locked. The sound of the gates closing down brought finality to William, realizing that here he will pay for the taste of power and freedom he shared with Mandy.

This is lock down, but it does not mean lights out. For some the cells mean safekeeping, for others freedom. One thing was for certain: Lockdown means you have to make it through the night. The huge yellow spotlights strategically

Chapter 10

mounted on the prison roof and walls light up the yard. There is not a soul in sight, not even one prison guard can be seen. The smell of dagga fills the place as various inmates lights up. He can see through the gate as prisoners are taking out food smug-gled from the day, pork chops, bread, simba chips, drugs. Some are making coffee. Various radios are playing, each a different channel. On one is a christian station another hip hop.

Some prisoners are writing letters, other reading bible, most busy talking gang business. He overhears the hard slam of a person being disciplined by other prisoners, the scream of the man's voice echoes through the cell but everyone continues as if it is normal. Keys are heard, and the guards enter the yard, walking past the cells barely looking inside. Here and there a prisoner talks to the guard, and as quick as they entered the yard they leave again. Moments later the lights of the cells are all turned off. But not all are ready for bed. There are still drugs to be smoked and dealt, sex to be had, threats to be delivered, and prayers to be made. "Master locked" the guard shouts. It reminded him of his days at boarding school.

He is inside the small cell with 6 men inside. The prisoners carefully look at him *"Gee 'n skuif"* (give me a cigarette), the first prisoner demands William moving closer threatening. He shakes his head and turns away. He looks around to see if there are any guards, but there is none visible at present. The prisoner tap him on the shoulder. He turns around and hit the man in the chest hurling him between the steel bunk beds. Their eyes were fixed on each other. He knew that night he should not sleep, as this cell might be his death bed. Trying to keep your eyes open brings back many memories. William sees Mandy, her eyes, the Namib desert.

The loud sound of steel keys unlocking the prison door can be heard loudly. The guard enters and looks at William, unscathed, surprising. The guard looks at William *"Klagtes?"* (complaints?). The prisoners looks around and shake their head. The guards turns around and leave. The inmate William hit in chest walks past William. William hold him back for moment. *"Sorry"* William says to the prisoner in a soft voice, giving a cigarette to the man without the others seeing.

> *"I did not come to prison to make friends, nor be reformed.*
> *But I knew I had to find a way to survive if I wanted to see Mandy",*
> William thought to himself.

He follows the other prisoners to a courtyard where they are allowed their daily exercise. A few are kicking ball, others are talking in groups, smoking, dealing with guards secretively, others do push ups. It seems peaceful in a strange way. A prisoner walks past William, takes off a sock that has a lock inside and he swings it aggressively at another inmates head. He hits the man against the head. The man drops to the floor, dead. The guards grabs the man and pulls him back William standing next to the man bleeding bends down. The man has no pulse. The prisoner William gave the cigarette to earlier stands next to him staring at a familiar sight, death. *"My broe, moenie kom speel nie"* (this is not a playing turf), the prisoner says. William stands up and turns around. In the corner of his eyes he see the various prisoners assessing him, talking. One man in specific, Ricardo, takes immediate distaste in him.

"Hey jey. whitey! Wies jey in die vierhoeke?" (Hey white boy! Who are you in pris-on?), Ricardo says. He turns away trying not to get into confrontation. *"Jey Frans? Dis nie jou ma se huis hierie nie!"* (This is not your mothers house), Ricardo says wanting to provoke William. Ricardo pokes him in the chest and face him straight in the eyes. *"Ek sal jou dood lem jou naai"* (I will stab you to death), Ricardo says. Other prisoners laughing at the back understanding the predicament he finds himself in here. He grabs Ricardo's hand and force him to the ground instantly. Ricardo breaks Ricardo's hand and the scream can be heard. Other prisoners stand closer and he knows that he is by far outnumbered here. The alarm bells sound just in time as the guards try and break up the scuffle. The guard angrily escorts

William and the furious and humiliated Ricardo away. *"Jy's mince hoor jy my"* (You are mince meat you hear me), Ricardo says as he is taken to the medical room William is forcefully taken down long passage, away from the other prisoners to block C. *"Ons het genoeg moeiliheid hier! Ons soek nie nog nie. Verstaan jy?"* (We have enough trouble here. Do you understand?), the guard says to him.

The guard locks the cell door and walks away. He examines the cell. There is a steel toilet, a basin, a couple of blankets rolled up in the corner. The walls are covered with gang slogans, and a filthy smell of urine, blood and pine-gel used to clean the place. Prison life felt like his training days, except hostility came from all sides.

Each day the prisoners had an hour of recreational time. Recreation being an odd phrasing choice. Apart from usual exercise routines and sports, some of the guards were dealing drugs to the prisoners. Information was their form of currency. It paid well to be a snitch. But their life insurance policy wasn't up to flack. It wasn't long before he caught the attention of the unsavory sort in the form of Ricardo. His frame was sinuous, lank and his colored skin was canvased in DIY tattoo's.

"Hey jey whitey, wies jy in die vierhoeke?" (Hey whiteboy, who are you in these walls?) screams Ricardo. He ignores him and looks away. *"Praat jy frans? Hierd-ie's nie djo ma se huis nie!"* (Do you speak French? This ain't your mother's house!" continues Ricardo. *"Ek sal jou lem. Moenie my so eyeball nie. Hoor jy vanilla?"* (I'll stab you. Don't you look at me. You understand vanilla?) Ricardo shoves William, but before he could pull out a shiv the guards were on them, beating down on them with their batons before escorting them away at gunpoint towards solitary confinement. The first time was always the worst for any inmate. For the next two weeks, all he could do in the two by two meter room was work out to keep his mind clear.

Time passed by quickly and he had his first visitor in months. Mandy sat on the other side of a thick pane of glass holding the phone to her ear waiting for him. They chat casually for a while before Mandy drops the mother of all bombs on William's head: *"Babe. I'm pregnant."* She tells him, already sobbing. *"That's fantastic!"* William felt giddy. *"How far along are you?"* Mandy sits for a moment without saying anything. *"Three months."* She finally says. This upset William: *"Why didn't you say anything before I was locked up?"* *"Because then you wouldn't have gone."* She says, crying. The guard behind him grabs the phone from his hand and slams it on the receiver. *"Visitation is now over."* As he grabs William, Mandy becomes erratic as she is led out by the guard on her side.

Of course, the news of Mandy's pregnancy didn't sit well with his mother. She was heavily insistent the two marry as to avoid the shame of having her grand-child be born out of wedlock. The ceremony itself was of the shotgun variety, with William, Mandy, his mother along with Jason, a few guards and the priest present to go over the ordeal.

Mandy was dressed in white and her belly was swelling with each passing day.

Time passes on and visitation time comes around again. Jason sits across from William. The air was tense between the two. Jason was uncharacteristically quiet. Since his marriage, He had joined the Numbers gang in order to gain credibility. *"Why so quiet, Jason?"* asks an irritated William. *"It's nothing. I just came to see how you were doing. Mandy's fine. It seems like the date is almost here."* Jason answers sheepishly. *"Is she doing alright? Is she coping?"* he asks but Jason doesn't answer. *"I have to go. I don't want to leave mom and Mandy alone for too long."*

Something didn't sit right with him. As Jason left he was escorted to the mess hall. Back with his gang, he looked around and saw Ricardo, on the far side of the room, looking at him and gesturing towards him while whispering in the ear of his subordinate. *"Hier kom kak."* (Here comes trouble) said Kenwyn, the man who initiated William into the gang.

Ricardo stood from his table along with other members of his gang and before the guards could react the two factions were at each other with all sorts of shivs and shanks and anything that could be sharpened into a point. The brawl became so intense the guards pulled out of the area and dropped heavy duty gas grenades amidst the mad crowd. When the smoke cleared, all inmates were escorted back to their cells save for William, who found himself bloodied inside solitary confinement.

After his stint in solitary, William's mother came to visit her son. Still bruised, he sat down across from his mother at the table. She seemed concerned. *"Mom? Where's Mandy? Is she alright? How's my son?"* he asks. *"It's not easy to say this, Will. Mandy and Jason..."* she starts. *"What about Mandy and Jason?"* he interrupts. *"Well, they're living together. They've been living together for while now. As a couple."* The silence grows heavy. Paper scratching the table as his mother hands him divorce proceedings sound like nails on a chalkboard. *"It'd be easier if you just signed, Will."* William stays silent. His mother looks at him for a long while before finally being escorted away by the guards. He stays seated at the table. All he can hear is white noise, staring at the papers in front of him.

CHAPTER 11

An old man was reading the bible in the cell next to William's and then carving it into the wall. He was sitting in his cell and looking at the photo of his baby boy. He struggles as he sees memories of himself with Mandy as it is ruined with memories of Jason. *"Can you stop scratching for God's sake."* Shouts William. He looks through the prison bar, the old man is quiet. *"Old man, please, I am begging you."* replies William. *"It is for God's sake I keep carving."* tells the man. *"Fantastic."* Says William sarcastically. The old man looks at William. *"There is but one way, the eye is the lamp of the soul. When your eye is good, your body is filled with light. When your eyes are bad, darkness, absolute darkness. Your eyes are not completely dark yet."* Answers the old man. He shakes his head and the man smiles and continues scribbling. William tears a page from the bible and makes a cigarette.

It was visiting day and to some that meant seeing loved ones, for others it was getting a parcel with cigarettes or food. Then, the soul of the prison takes its first breathe for the day, and gun shots fill the air. Prisoners fall to the ground and take cover while others rush to the barred windows to feast on the action. In the court yard are two armed prisoners running between the cells trying to open doors to hide and take cover. They had just overpowered two police officers who were loading awaiting trial prisoners to take them to court and had taken their service pistols from them.

The two prisoners were frantic with confusion and fear, as they realize they had run through the wrong doors and are now trapped in a different section of prison instead of being outside. From behind the steel door more shots are fired from more officers and the prisoners return fire. Armed men can be seen on top of the roof, while two snipers take their positions. Hundreds of voices are filling the air as prisoners cheer their comrades on, giving advice, yielding warnings, and pointing out the enemy. The armed convicts fire at the roof and at the gate. Shots are returned with automatic weapons.

One prisoner throws his firearm from him and lies face down in the middle of the courtyard. The second begins to climb the wall by a water pipe and reaches the roof. At that moment, he decides to surrender and lifts his hands in the air, a shot from the one sniper is fired. The prisoner drops dead from the roof. Suddenly the courtyard is filled with armed men pointing their firearms at the prisoner who had surrendered.

Due to the commotion, visitation was canceled. Outside the prison walls stood my mother along with other visitors who had heard the gunfire. Meanwhile, we were stripped naked in the courtyard and searched thoroughly for any concealed weapons.

William is busy pumping iron in the outdoor gym. His muscles gleam with sweat. He pushes the weights up and down like a man possessed. A group of men watch him from a distance. A thin-faced, tattoo covered man joins them, known as TAT. *"Dis die man wat Ricardo soek. Hy dink hy's 'n ndota. Maak hom 'n hond"* (That's the man. He fancies himself a king. Make a dog out of him), the prisoner says to a large sized man, covered in gang tattoos.

The man gives Tat a small piece of rolled up newspaper. Something is rolled up inside out of sight of the others. William was preparing for a boxing match, the entertainment of the guards and prisoners alike. It was good for morale and got the blood flowing in a controlled way they believed, a type of unreported gladiator sport.

The sun slowly sets over the four corners of the prison. Inmates gather. Money is being betted, by the prison wardens as well. The inmates are shouting frantic. A make shift boxing ring stands in the middle of the yard.

William places on his boxing gloves. He gets into his corner. Its been a long time since his first fight, but he has putter many men down since that day. On the other side is TAT

Ricardo is holding his hand and looks at Tat and nod his head. Tat puts something inside his boxing gloves. He dance around the man as the man tries to punch him. Tat pushes him against the corner and before the guard comes closer hits William against the head with the boxing glove, the sound of the shank against his skull can be heard. William drops down to the floor, his head bleeding. Tat kicks William as he is lying. William crawls onto his knees, a buzzing sound filling the space, slightly out of focus sight of the other prisoners. He can see Kenwyn shouting towards him. The sound is all blocked out and everything is happening slowly, as blood drips around him. William moves quickly as Tat hits towards the floor, hitting a hole into the wooden floor. He hook Tat with a shot against the jaw and then another. Tat drops down.

"Staan op, maak hom klaar" (Stand up and finish him), Ricardo shouts angrily Tat is cold out, no movement at all. A prison guard checks on Tat and walk to William, lifting his arms in the air. Ricardo angrily gives out money to his victors, he lost the bet, even more he lost respect.

Four years later...

William sat waiting for the parole board, practicing his speech over and over. The men enter and William stands to greet them before taking his seat again. *"Hoe gaan dit vandag, Austen?"* (How are you today, Austen?) asks the Parole officer. The man was looking at William's file. He looks around before finally answering. *"Dit gaan goed meneer, en met meneer?"* (Very well, sir. And with sir?) replies William. The same questions echo through the room. *"Wil jy huistoe gaan?"* (Do you want to go home?) questions the parole officer. He nods his head. *"Ek wil meneer, Ek wil Asseblief."* (I do sir. Please, I do) says William. The man looks at him and puts his hand forward. *"Gee my jou kaartjie."* (Your card please) states the officer. The man takes his prisoner ID card and writes a parole date on it. He hands it back. William looks at it and tries to hide his excitement.

William walked back to his cell, trying hard not to share the joy. Keeping the date a secret from the others, not going to let anyone take it away. William walks to the phones and calls his mother, he puts his hand over his ear to block out the noise. *"I have good news, I got my date to come home."* says William. *"That's wonderful news. When's the date?"* questions Merissa. *"Next week."* Answers William. Merissa was silent for a while then answers. *"Just keep in mind that things... have changed. Mandy and Jason..."* She stops herself before saying something to upset William further. *"I have a house in Hermanus, you can live with me until you find your feet."*

Merissa says to William.

I was out of jail, but in no way free, I was given a car. I lived in a nice house on the beach. Mandy refused to return my calls or even let me speak to my son. I started doing drugs to cope and dealt with gangs to sustain my habit. On the day of my son's birthday, I thought that surprising him would be the best choice.

Crawling up the driveway in a white Ford Ranchero 5.4Litre V8 was William. He stops in front of the house, engine roaring. William climbs out with a present. Jason sees through the gate and excuses himself from the friends. William's son approaches Jason excited about the car. *"Can I drive in that car?"* asks the boy. Jason sends him to go play and approaches him. *"I came to see my boy."* Says William. Jason blocks his view. *"I don't think it is a good time for you to see him."* Answers Jason. *"With you there is never a good time!"* Shouts William. *"I think it is better that you leave, please."* Says Jason.

Mandy peers through the house window, watching William. *"I just traveled one and a half thousand kilometers to see my boy!"* screams William. *"I understand but…"* starts Jason. *"No matter what you say, he is still my son."* Answers William. *"We are just tired of your trouble Will."* Sighs Jason. *"I am tired of this nonsense, it has been six years of me being in jail while you raised my son, you sleep with her behind my back and take my kid. Can't you see I am trying really hard."* Screams William. Jason shakes his head, William pushes Jason. *"Today is his birthday and I brought him a present."* Says William. *"If you don't leave, I will call the police."* Jason says to William. *"You stole all that is dear to me and treat me like I am the monster. You were my brother Jason."* Sobs William. Jason turns and walks towards the door. *"If there is a God up there, I hope he can forgive you. Because God knows I can't do it."* Cries William walking away. William gets in the car and drives away.

William was sitting between various gangsters, high as a kite. He was seated on a torn recliner, smoking a mixture of different drugs and drinking whiskey. He had a tattoo of a sword on his upper arm, with the inscription; 'EVEN THOUGH I GO THROUGH THE VALLEY OF THE SHADOW OF DEATH I WILL FEAR NO EVIL'. Lights were flashing, music deafening. William was watching one girl in particular. She walks up to William. *"You wanna drag?"* asks William. The girl takes it from him and takes a deep breath. She blows it over his lips. She sits on his lap and touches him. *"You got cash?"* she asked. He nodded. The girl whispered in his ear and softly bit it. William puts money down her pants. She takes him by the hand and walks to another room. Alex walks to him, who is lying naked next to the prostitute. He shakes himself awake. He gets dressed and takes his firearm and his money back from the passed-out girl.

A boat pulls into the shoreline, under the cover of the sea mist. William keeps an eye out for the crew as they load the masses of abalone into a van. *"Chase al daai pearlies, bruitjie. Me mos like the Jesus gang with the miracle of fishes."* Says Alex. *"Don't feel like getting crucified tonight, so keep it down."* Alex smiles as he continues loading abalone. Alex pays William in a thick stack of money. William immediately spends all his cash on drugs. *"Don't blow your wad, bru. You still owe the gang a lot of money for the last three months. Kenwyn's been covering for you, but Ricardo is out."* William looks around anxious. *"And you're pissing in his yard."* Says Alex. William nods his head and turns away.

A middle-aged man dressed in a suit stands urinating into a urinal. He finishes and turns zipping his pants and walks to the basins. He opens the tap and rinses his hands. Closes the tap and dries his hands. Suddenly William appears in the mirror behind him. The man turns around and notices a knife in William's hand. *"Your wallet and your phone."* Yells William. *"Please don't hurt me, I have a wife and kids."* cries the handing over the phone and wallet. William then puts a knife against the man's throat. *"You don't move, understand."* Says William. The man nods and William runs out of the bathroom.

He was walking on the way to the drug house. A car creeps slowly behind him. He increases his pace, without deliberately breaking into a run. Next thing the blinding lights of an idling car block his path. Shadowy figures approach him, dragging a shovel along the ground. The group parts and Ricardo appears holding the shovel. *"Thought I smelt an old dog."* Taunts William. Two other gang-sters point guns at him. Ricardo tosses the shovel to the ground and William picks it up and starts digging.

Then suddenly without warning, William spins around, launching a spade full of dirt in the faces of his assailants. He manages to take out two of the henchmen with the shovel. And as he clambers out of the hole, he's faced with the barrel of a gun pointed at him by Ricardo. He grins viciously and is about to pull the trigger, when another gangster stops him. *"Kenwyn said don't use guns."*

He looks up and didn't wait another second. He runs full pace. Navigating through the crowded streets, trying to stay out of sight. His pace was not towards something. But rather his urgency was to get away from something, or someone. His shirt splattered with blood, whose blood was only known to those that chased him. An unsavory group of abalone and drug traders known as the "Numbers". And not far behind him was Ricardo desperately chasing after William like a rabid hound. William turns a corner and pushes himself in an awkward and potentially lethal position. He stood between his pursuers and a High-Wire fence he couldn't scale fast enough. He bends over breathing hard, Ricardo steps into the road, gang members all around. Brandishing knives. His heart beats in his ear like a war drum as he says: *"What do they say? It's not the size of the dog in a fight, but the size of the fight in the dog. And now the Devil's Dance."*

Chapter 11

William Austen

CHAPTER 12

William bursts through the front door of Kenwyn's place, Kenwyn is sitting there, a girl busy dancing on his lap. Kenwyn shakes his head at William. *"Jy moet vlieg nou of hulle knip jou vlerke morsaf."* (You need to flee or they'll cut your wings) says Kenwyn. William nods his head and throws clothing into a bag. *"Hul is oppad hierheen."* (They are on their way here) William looks at Kenwyn. *"Thanks, I owe you."* William grabs the car keys, Kenwyn shakes his head and he walks past his car.

He is walking down the street, careful of every car he sees. He starts to run, weaving between the trees, He pants for breath, straining his lungs as he deepens his stride, running until his muscles burnt acid. Ricardo was still looking for him. Their car was packed with gangsters with guns, knives and machetes. Ricardo and his gang burst through the doors. Kenwyn was busy kissing the girl on the couch. Kenwyn turns around and sternly looks at Ricardo.

The parking area was jammed with holiday makers. The petrol attendants had their hands full with travelers lined up to refill their vehicles. Customers exit the Steers with burgers and drinks like busy ants. Some barely manage to carry all the snacks they have acquired for the journey. William was passing through. He has grown a beard. He is tanned and lost some weight. He walks to the public phones and does not look people in the eyes. He picks up the phone.

Seated on the couch watching a movie was Jason, Mandy and William's son when the phone rings. *"Get the phone."* Asks Jason. The boy gets up and walks to the phone. "Hello" replies the Boy. William wants to talk but can't. *"Hello, anybody there?"* calls the boy. He holds the phone. Eyes clamped shut. Tears flow. He puts the phone back on the receiver, and walks into the distance. The sun begins to set behind him.

Heavy rain pours down, as William walks the streets of Hillbrow aimlessly, a lost man. He approaches a group of prostitutes and smiles weakly at one particular woman who catches his eye. The woman walks and touches William, searching his pockets. *"You don't have cash?"* says the prostitute. The prostitute looks at him disgusted. *"I got cash."* The prostitute slides up to him seductively. She touches his chest, he coughs. *"I got to make a call, be right back. All right?"* replies William. The prostitute walks away. William puts a few coins in and dials a number. *"Evening."* greets Mandy. *"Mandy, I just want to…"* starts William. *"William?"* asks Mandy. *"Yes."* There is a quiet moment, he can hear Mandy crying softly. *"Don't cry, I just want to speak to my son. Just once, I beg of you."* pleads William.

"William. Listen to me. He doesn't even know you. The only memory he has of you is you showing up with your flashy car, which really impressed him. And throwing his father to the floor." Sobs Mandy. *"I am his father, I have a right to see him."* Says William. *"Jason has been around, Jason knows him. William listen to me, if you want to be good to him, to us, leave us alone."* Cries Mandy. William doesn't reply. *"Take care of yourself Will."* Mandy hangs up the phone, William is broken. He wanders the streets in shock. All the faces, the noises, blur into one big surreal nightmare. In a half-lit corner, a shadowy figure seems to be staring at him. William swallows and quickens his step. William glances behind him nervously. It seems the man is following him. He runs, but the man doesn't follow.

He is sitting on the floor, going through old photos. He tosses them onto an already growing pile and lights up a joint. Then sets the pile on fire. Staggering to his feet, he presses play on the stereo and dances to the music wildly, smashing into furniture and pulling down bookcases. There are photos all around him of himself, Jason and Mandy. He burns the photos. Eventually, he staggers to a drawer, pulling out a gun and kneels down in the middle of the room. William moves the revolver up and down in his mouth banging against the top and bottom rows of teeth. He closes his eyes. Tears flowing. He is about to pull the trigger. *"If there really is a God."* he asks.

He owers his gun and reaches out for a last cigarette. *"A last smoke before the curtain call."* William laughs. The cigarette box is empty. *"Great, just when you need a friend, they are gone."* Says William. He throws the box to the side. He picks up coins tossed over the floor. He counts it. He gets to his feet. He places the gun in the cupboard. He looks at gun. *"I will be back and I know you have heard this before, but count on me, I have nowhere else to go."* He laughs in his high state of mind.

He walks in the café, heading for the counter. He avoids eyes contact with the woman behind the counter. *"A single cigarette and a box of matches."* Asks William. For a moment, the girl looks like Mandy. He twitches his eyes. The girl gives him the cigarette and he walks away. He exits the shop with a box of matches and a cigarette in his hand. He strikes the match and lights the smoke. The woman from the shop follows him. *"Excuse me. You are William, right?"* She asks, friendly. William looks around awaiting a trap of some kind. *"That's me."* William takes another drag of his cigarette. *"I would like to introduce you to a friend of mine."* He looks around. *"Now?"* asks William. The Woman nods her head. *"Won't take more than a minute."*

He follows her toward her house which is situated on the same premis-es. She takes him by the arm. He uncomfortably pulls back. Inside is a man dressed in what seems like army gear. The man looks at William intensely. There is complete silence. The man smiles and starts speaking right away. *"You know He loves you right? My name is Chris"* says Chris. William looks around. *"Jesus loved you so much that He gave His life so you can live for free."* States Chris. William shakes his head and wants to turn around. *"Do you at least know who Jesus is?"* asks Chris. *"The son of God right?"* answers William.

Chris looks deep into William's eyes. *"Everything you have done... your addic-tions... all of it. He forgives You and want to give you a chance, to fix this mess."* He stands unsure. Chris goes a step closer to William and hold him in his arms. *"The Bible says that we have all sinned and fallen short of God's glory, and that the wages of sin are death. But God loves us all so much that He sent Jesus to save us from ourselves. JOHN tells us that while we were yet sinners, God died for us. If you confess with your mouth the Lord Jesus and believe in your heart that God has raised Him from the dead, you will be saved. For whoever calls upon the Name of The Lord shall be saved."*

After that day, William cleaned himself up and threw away his drugs. He starts Bible study and gets baptized in the ocean. He struggles to fit in the church and has withdrawal symptoms but still he pursues God. While driving through Hillbrow, he looks up to the Vodacom tower with its flickering lights. A beacon point for junk-ies. It's higher than all the buildings around it. Everywhere he looks are Nigerians, dealing drugs, and pimping. A few Metro police vehicles are doing their scheduled patrols, but appear to be minding their own business. William feels sad, burdened. He pulls to the side of the road and switches off the engine. He moves the rear-view mirror, and catches his reflection: *"Don't do it William. Don't buy."*

Immediately he is approached by a dealer. *"Hey boss, what do you want? The usual?"* asks the dealer. William stares at him for a moment, then signals with a wave that he is not buying. The dealer walks around the car checking the number plate, and then looks back at him, as if to warn him. Across the street a man hands a Nigerian a pack of notes. The dealer counts it and hands the man a plastic pouch. Without checking the parcel, the buyer wraps his hand tightly around it and walks away quickly disappearing around the building anxious to get out of the eye and desperate to use. Sounds of people in the dark ally, maybe its sounds of demons. Strange ghostly forms appear and disappear. Barefoot children sit on the pavement, sniffing glue, surviving with a hell of a lot of pain. William looks upon these scenes of shame, hell and misery, starts the car and drives away. Tears roll down his cheeks. Hurting for all the broken people. He knows what it is like living in that hell, and how he had almost returned. Frustrated, he grips the steering tightly with both hands, jerking it, shouting. Almost attempting to break it out from the car. William stops next to the road and look up to the sky. *"You say you came to set the captives free Lord, set me free."* Says William before driving off.

The N1 highway stretches far across the landscape. In the distance, a few trucks can be seen heading towards this significant land mark. William sighs, picks up the cell phone and dials. *"Jason it's me, please don't hang up."* Jason is shocked and remains quiet for the moment. *"William are you okay?"* asks Jason. *"I am good."* Says William. *"Mom told me you sound different, that you stopped using drugs."* *"That's right. I…"* starts William. He collects himself. *"I had an encounter… with Jesus".* There is silence on the other end. *"I have been running too long, fighting… I can't anymore Jason. I need you to listen."* States William. *"I am listening."* Answers Jason. "

"Jason, I have hurt you, mom and Mandy terribly. I want you to forgive me." Cries William. *"I am the one who should say sorry William I…"* William grips the phone and wipes his eyes. *"You are a good father to my son, and a husband to Mandy. I know that in my heart. Thank you for protecting them… I forgive you"* says William. The line is quiet. Both Jason and William are attentive and emotional. *"You are my brother Jason… and I love you. That's all I wanted to say".* Jason is all emotional, never think-

ing he would hear these word from his brother.

"William... let me know when you want to come visit. I, we will all want to see you." "Will love to, but I need to make things straight in the Cape... I don't know how things are going to turn out. So if anything happens to me... tell my son" sobs William. "You come tell him... alright. We will keep you in prayer. Nothing will happen alright." Answers Jason. William smiles for the first time in a while. He hangs up. Night is beginning to fall; the illuminated cross grows brighter with the impending darkness. He glances up and smiles. Whatever lies ahead, he and his brother are finally free. Two trucks pass by blowing their horns. William waves.

Some might say there was no need to go back... but I had to face my ghosts or I would never be free. I believed somehow that God was with me.

The township throbs with energy as people make their way through the bustling streets, and vendors sell their wares. William's old V.W. winds its way through familiar alley ways. A few people recognize him, pointing and waving. Eventually the car pulls up outside the dealer's yard. William sits in the car, weighing up his options. He glances at the cars parked outside the yard, and notices Ricardo's Corolla. And at the gate of the yard are two gang members, the watchmen. William moves across the road, holding up his hands to show he is not armed.

"Naai..kyk wie is hier" (Look who's here) shouts the man. "Kenwyn. Come check this out!" Kenwyn comes out of the house followed by five of his men. "Ek dog jy's dood. Waar kom jy vandaan?" (thought you were dead. Where are you coming from?) asks Kenwyn. William hugs Kenwyn. "You won't believe it, my old friend." Smiles William. "We were talking about you yesterday... we need some hands on the boat, shipping. But some here wants your blood." "I came to make things right." Answers William. Kenwyn looks at William unsure what he means but takes William inside. "Stick close my brother. Now is not the best time." The group head inside. In the darkest corner of the room, sitting on a couch is Ricardo, glaring at him. His hand is on a pistol, tucked into his pants. "Hosh! Nwala hier's ndota."

The house goes quiet. Some are excited to see him, and immediately walk up to him greeting him. Others give death stares, whilst the rest couldn't care less. "Sit down." States Kenwyn. William sits down in the chair, which is next to Kenwyn's.

A silence slowly settles over the room. Ricardo and two of his gang get to their feet, beer in hand. Ricardo is burning with anger. *"You take me for a fool to come in here."* Ricardo approaches William aggressively, hand on his pistol. William hesitates a moment then clears his throat. All eyes are on him. Kenwyn nods for him to continue. *"I found the Lord and I am done with these things."* replies William. There is a moment of awkward silence, then Ricardo bursts out laughing. Several people join Ricardo in mocking William.

Kenwyn quickly gets between them, pressing his palm against Ricardo's chest. *"Minute... ndota! Die man noem hy wil sake regmaak laat hom praat"* (Give him a chance to speak.) Ricardo looks over Kenwyn's shoulder glaring at William. *"Will jy vandag bloed trek hier, in my huis?"* (You want to draw blood in my house today?) Kenwyn asks Ricardo. No one is moving, the tension is clear. Hands are close to the sides, wether a blade or a gun, the moment was eager for blood. Eventually Ricardo backs off, returning to his darkened couch. *"Nou praat"* (so talk), Ricardo says, irritated that his authority is challenged. William hesitates a moment then clears his throat.

All eyes are on him. Kenwyn nods for him to continue. *"My legs were strong for the Numbers. You know. But I couldn't carry it no more. I had to give it to God"* William says looking around the room. *"Get lost. Don't come preach here"*, Ricardo says angrily. *"I came to make things right, to pay back and pray so you can also be free"* William says. *"Bid se gat, jy skuld my geld, of die bloed sal loop"*, Ricardo says furious (to hell with prayer, you owe me money, or blood will flow today). Kenwyn *"Hoeveel kroon is daai?"* (how much does he owe you?). *"Nog R2000"* Ricardo says. William gets to his feet, putting his hand slowly into his jacket pocket. Several people respond aggressively, think he is reaching for a gun. He removes a brown envelope, and walks slowly towards Ricardo.

"Hiers jou krone" (Here's your money) William says as he gives the envelope over. Ricardo snatches it, rips the envelope open, removes the notes and begins to count. Satisfied that it is the right amount, he pockets the money. Then he slowly gets to his feet, face to face with William, their eyes locked. Our paths have locked many times, but this is the last. I am sorry for the wrong I did to you, William says looking Ricardo in the eyes, with a sense of grace in the midst of all the tension.

Chapter 12

"*Kyk hier, ek wil mos jou vol gate maak. Jou gefret change*" (I want to shoot you full of holes, change your face), Ricardo says still angered and unsure what to make of the situation. Ricardo puts his gun away inches pocket with the envelope.

"*Maar somehow kan ek nie. Miskien is die God saam jou*" (somehow I can't. Maybe this God is with you). Every one laughs. The tension is relieved. Ricardo sticks his hand out. William immediately takes hold of it. Kenwyn closes his eyes. The others look at him strangely. "*Nou bid*" (now pray) Kenwys says.

William says to himself ,relieved, *"thank you Jesus"*.

William prays a simple prayer.

CHAPTER 13: EPILOGUE

"Jesus, you are Lord. What authority or power can compare with you? Yet you love us so much. So much so that you didn't just talk about it. You did something about it. You took a nail for each and every one of us, bled on a cross for the sins of the world. And by your stripes we are healed. I pray for my brothers, for Kenwyn, for Linden and for every gang member here. Every addict, every person in this room. Forgive them their sins. Wash them in your Blood. Save their souls. Protect them every day of their lives. Amen." Prays William.

The hall is jam-packed with prisoners. Seated among them are about twenty prison guards including the Head of the Prison. The prisoners open their eyes. *"So, as you've just heard, I was a pretty wild guy. But just like me, your lives are not over. There is hope. Jesus knows everything about you. Regardless of what you have done He loves you. His Blood, His Power and His Love are here for you right now, just as it was for me that day."* Answers William. The room erupts with cheers, whistles and clapping, as the crowd stands to its feet.

After that the coffee shop was packed with patrons. To the back of the coffee shop, there were several tables joined, occupied by members of different churches and ministries. Among the group is William. On William's left is Christa. She is a beautiful with sparkling green eyes, filled with life and purity. William shares a bit of his testimony and then Christa shares about the ministry she is involved with. As she speaks, he is captured by the beauty of her soul. He glances at her almost lovingly. The moment is however disrupted by Gerhard, the event organizer as he gets to his feet. *"Thank you all for your time. Hope you enjoyed the meeting as much as I have. See you all next week same time."* Says Gerhard.

He and Christa both get to their feet at the same time. *"It was so nice meeting you."* replies William. They smile at each other. *"I would love to hear the rest of your testimony."* Asks Christa. *"I would be glad to share...but it's not an easy story."* What started as a mere sharing of his testimony soon became a lifetime friendship. Long conversations and both coming from a place of brokenness with a desire to help others soon led to a close and deep connection. A few months later, Christa and William got married. It was not a big occasion due to financial constrains. Everything this time felt so different, he opened himself up to feel again and to be loved. It was indeed a scary space to be in, the idea of losing what was so dear to him once again came up time and time again with Christa comforting me and reassuring me about her love.

He was married now, but God still had a plan for him. He knew in his heart that God called him... and felt that he had to go to the Freestate, to Parys, to share His good news and his story. William shared at schools, prisons and church-es. He was given accommodation and food, and kindness. But then one day it all changed for William when he walked into the house with flowers for Christa.

He walks to Christa and kisses her. She smiles broad and he notices. Christa takes the pregnancy test from behind her back. He smiles and picks her up, swings her around out of joy, and then carefully put her down. He places his hands over her tummy. Over time they started preparing their home for their baby.

With his wife sick and far along her pregnancy, William rarely got any sleep. Between his concern for his wife and child's wellbeing, and a festering boulder of guilt strapped upon his back. His lot in life, he felt, was to finally be over-taken by the worries of the world. Often during his sleepless nights, he'd allow himself to think about Jason, and Mandy and the son who would never call him father for the rest of his days.

Out in the dark paths and alleyways, the boys were stalking pray like a pack of starving jackals. Their unified attire called to mind the gangs of that respected town, and the usual initiation practice involved a barbaric practice: Find and kill at least one drunkard. With unflinching willingness, the hoodlums scoured the night, looking not for a victim, but a golden ticket straight into the gang's good graces.

The little boy is born and he holds him in his arms, still breathing, Samuel is born a healthy baby boy. This was a big moment for William, not having had this experience with the birth of his child with Mandy. That was time that was robbed from him whilst he was doing his sentence behind the cold prison bars. He was not going to let anything take it away from him again. He adored the young boy, being very protective, praying early mornings on his knees.

It brought a new stronger bond between them as a family, but even the strongest bonds are tested with time. He relied on donations from his outreaches and did not wanted to be a burden on people. It was a difficult place as William was able to get his hands on all kinds of money and resources in his previous way of life. The path of the righteous was indeed a test of endurance daily.

He sat on the concrete step which led to main door of the church. Loosen-ing his tie, he takes a deep breath and exhales into the lazy wind blowing from his back, pushing the troubled sigh away from a defeated him.

Somewhere on the other side, a place akin to a shanty town, riddled with tin-roof shacks and the only source of drinkable located on the far end of a walk through cold, miserable July weather. The drunken stupors of most of the shabeen's regulars seem to have been amplified by a cold carrier wind. Outside, in a dark alley, a group of rowdy youths take turns huffing an unidentifiable substance from a crumpled brown paper bag. The rush they receive from this practice seems as rec-reational at first, but with a simple hand gesture and an ego-centric stride, the lads were off to cause all manner of mischief.

Our struggle continued. Jason got sick and for all that happened between us, he was still my brother. Our mission didn't fare much better either. Pastors in Parys had no interest in letting me share my story. William never really felt accepted by the church elders at any of the gatherings. Old-school, pompous windbags with conservative sticks rammed far up the balloon-knot. His gruff, tattooed visage helped to steer away the only people with the influence to have others listen to his sermons. I was once again an outsider, even by those who I called brother and sister in Christ. I could see the hurt in the community, mothers struggling with their sons and daughters getting stuck in a lifecycle of drugs, early pregnancy or just a need for something more, a touch of God beyond the children bible story version. The need was real I could sense it, but it was clear from the concern of the elders that I had no place speaking to their congregation.

I was frustrated to say the least, being shunned like this. Standing outside was a Muslim man. He came from Cape Town. I greeted him and we began to speak about God. I told him what I believe in and what I am doing in Parys, I also told him how hard it was, especially here. I will never forget his words, he said; *"You do what you have come to do."* I did not expect that from a man of a different faith. We connected in that moment, beyond our belief being different.

The coming months tested his resilience. The rejections became fewer, but acceptance within the more conservative communities still eluded him. Still, William preached where he could. Spreading his message to all souls alike, the downtrodden and the desperate. Every face William made a point to remember, the features etched onto their faces of turbulent pasts. With each passing sermon, the purpose became clearer. But even these fleeting events passed, William's wish to reach a larger crowd remained unobtainable.

Months grew wider between each sermon; the winters grew cold as William's hope began to dwindle. Sitting alone in his living room; his wife and child sound asleep. He became lost within the memories he built up without regard to caution. He thought of his old gang mates; the angry spitting faces of prison guards and drill sergeants and his lost beloved Mandy. Simpler times that quickly boiled away into a chaotic field of discontent for anyone and anything in his path. His callous attitude towards his mother, and the absence of his father. These thoughts crept around his head as he sat by himself in the dimly lit quarters. It was a war inside his head.

Crime within the inner cities began to escalate, jobs became rarer and money scarcer. William still lacked the support he needed, and the stress was showing prominently. Walking with his family in the supermarkets, he would slyly eye the entrance to the liquor shop every time they would pass it walking through the aisles. The thought come to his mind how easily he would before be able to generate the kind of money that would buy his son and wife material comfort, a better life. William, time and time again draws himself away from this, knowing that path led him nowhere and it is the devil provoking him, breaking him down. William had become more withdrawn and as a result, considered indulging in old habits and vices.

The entrance to the liquor store morphed into golden arches adorned with the faces and events that William locked away in the far spaces of his mind. One specific day, William and Christa went shopping. He was looking for a few things and Christa was looking for things for baby Samuel. His thoughts clearly was not with the items he was buying and something else was bothering and boiling inside. As he picks items he sees the price of them and sighs, till it becomes unbearable *"Let's just go home please."* Demands William. *"But William I need to get this for Samuel. I can't…"* protests Christa. He walks out of the shop towards the car. Trying to cool himself down looking over other families, fathers that fills the boot with shopping bags. This inability to completely provide for his family is a stake in Williams heart.

Christa comes out with Samuel, bringing 2 bags to the car. He throws them in back and close the boot. He remains quiet as they all get in as well as drive away. Christa felt the tension radiating from him, she puts her hand on his knee but he pulls away. *"Babe…"* Christa stopped mid-sentence as he clenched his jaw, making the muscles of his cheeks poke out intensely. *"…Please talk to me"* she continues. *"It's not good to keep your problems bottled up. I'm here for you. William speak to me, please."*

"Christa, stop. Not now." he finally speaks, his tone harsh and short tem-pered. It wasn't long before the uneasy silence was broken by old-fashioned spousal arguing. Their wailing eventually woke the baby in the back seat to incessant wailing, serving only as a megaphone to the couple's screaming match.

Tires screeched on the sun-faded tarmac leading up to their driveway. Without a pause of silence, he carries his baby boy into the front portal of their home and places him down gently, his whole body shaking feverishly with internal rage. He wipes the tears from the babe's face, kisses him on his soft forehead and in a huff storms towards the car. Christa grab onto his arm. *"William, please don't go. Don't do this to your family. I'm sorry, please stay!"* Christa bawls through stammering, tear soaked words of love and desperation. He doesn't stop, every muscle taught in his body as he stomps angrily towards the car. With a slam and a screech William raced out of Christa's teary vision.

He drove to the golf course, to get rid of his anger. He did not want to be in this dark place, especially not with those he loves. He has come a long way, changed so much, but somehow all felt like it was tumbling in again. He was swinging his golf club, furiously hitting the balls into the distance. He walks back into the bar and starts drinking again. It felt as if he could just let go for once, then tomorrow all will go back to normal, the struggle to survive repeats. All the words of rejection repeated in his head, demons of his past was difficult to suppress. Other men were sitting there, laughing together, drinking shots and beer. All too familiar to William, a world he once left behind. It will only be this once William said to himself over and again.

He felt bad about using the little money he was able to get for his family. It felt that his world was colliding into a dark pit. Unable to provide a safe world to Christa and Sam, to provide to their financial needs. He was angry at him-self, angry at the church men who rejected him. It all didn't seem to matter right now. Hours would pass by in minute-time as his able became decorated with tumbler glasses still filled with melted ice and diluted brownish liquid. Rich businessmen coming to the golf course look at him strangely. The security comes to him and whispers to him. He shakes his head and walks out. No time for a fight, especially with someone so inferior to himself. He was a fighter, a champ. He survived so many things and nothing was going to get him down.

Walking to his car he felt powerful, an urge that use to drive much of his life, a demon that devoured and stole so much from him already over the years. He sees the security guard writing down the details of his car and he spins away furiously. The open road stretches out in front of him. The feeling of putting his feet on the acceleration and feeling the car fly over the road, a feeling of freedom with the speed. The feeling of being unstoppable, unbreakable, yet somehow broken, empty and so fragile. The mix of emotions spin in his head, laughter, tears, anger.

Shaken and emotionally despondent, he struggles to keep his vehicle in a straight line on the road home. In this daze, he neglects to notice a car coming from across the intersection. The last sound he hears is the screech of rubber against the blackened road and an impact which flings him through the windshield and onto the road before him.

He lied on the ground, bloodied and broken and barely able to see through the blood collecting in his eyes. He reaches his hand towards the heavens, weeping bloodied tears. A hand stretches out and holds William's tightly. He looks to his right and sees a man, vaguely resembling his father. Before long, another hand takes his left. A woman's hand, a mother's hand. More hands appear from the void around William and slowly begin lifting him off the ground. The faces, blurred and tinted red are of youths who attended his past sermons, a homeless man pushed away from entering church, some rebellious youth kids, a woman who was found between men… the broken so to speak. It seemed to have been all a blur. It seemed that the "outcasts", the ones that William reached out to, were now helping him. The figures lift William from the two-lane blacktop and towards a brilliant light, warm and inviting. William closes his eyes, but the light pierces through his eyelids. Every conceivable sense blurs out, and William fades, motionless.

It was early morning in the hospital. Most of what happened was a blur to William. Flashing lights of the theatre, the voice of his wife, a battle between life and death they said. William slowly opens his eyes sitting in the hospital bed, drips in his arms and still influenced by the strong narcotics and tranquillisers.

I was in a lot of pain. But my biggest pain was that I had lost the battle. I had fallen. I had sinned against those I loved and God. I betrayed the very debts Jesus cleared in my life, William thought to himself

William looks down in shame. He can see little Samuel in the room looking at him. He tries to sit up as he hears more voices. The people who he ministered to in Parys, and people he interacted with came to see him. The people that others pushed away as outcasts, that were most often found outside of the walls of the church. The people he has been so passionate about making a difference to. It has indeed been a long journey to William but he realized in that moment that it is not the end of his story. God still was actively involved and had a purpose, with Williams mistakes and all.

"*All my life I tried to be strong, tried to be a somebody. But I realized however there is only one conclusion to every story. We all fall down. No matter how strong we are*" William says. It felt that he was not worthy of speaking any of His great words. An elderly man puts his arm around William and nods his head. Even in his state of pain William started sharing a message, as if it is something that came out from his deepest, something even beyond him. God can surely use even a rock, or a donkey it seems. "*His grace is sufficient for you, for His power is made perfect in our weakness. Therefore, I will boast all the more gladly about my weaknesses, so that Christ's power may rest on me. That is why, for Christ's sake, I delight in weaknesses, in insults, in hardships, in persecutions, in difficulties. For when I am weak, He makes me strong."*

Chapter 13: Epilogue

William Austen

WILLIAM AUSTEN'S PERSONAL TESTIMONY

"Who am I, Lord, that You love me, and have given Yourself for me?"

My name is William Austen, and I have been so very deep in the world. All my life I had mingled with this world which lies in wickedness. And I was certainly condemned with it. Following is a shortened version of my life. Of who and what I was before I met JESUS, and of how good GOD has been to me, and am sure, is, and will be to whosoever calls upon HIS NAME. My childhood was plagued with many problems. My biological father was a violent man. An alcoholic, a wife beater, and a drug addict. Fearing for her life, and that of her children, my mother decided to run from him. As soon as he knew our whereabouts, we would pack up and move. We were always on the run. My life as a child was filled with fear and insecurity. By the time I attended high school, I was psychologically and emotionally damaged. I couldn't make friends. My grades were very low. I was always in trouble because of fighting and stealing. Most of my standard eight year I was absent from school, hanging out with all the wrong kind of people. "With criminals."

In 1987, I was called up for two-year military service in the old South African defense force. I was sixteen at the time. It was a nightmare. It done me no good. In 1997, I was sentenced for seven years imprisonment for fraud and theft. Life in jail was like being in hell. No freedom. No rights. Mental oppression. Gang wars. Murders. Rape. Corrupt Prison officials. Loneliness. Fear. Lice. Dirty food. Diseases. Suicides. And, my wife who I was married to at that time divorced me, and married my brother. After spending four years in jail, I was released in May 2001. I had so many dreams. Dreams of bonding with my son. Dreams of having a normal career. A normal life. But quickly I realized none of them were coming true. The baggage I was carrying from the past years made it all impossible. I was still the same man. I was still friends with the greatest of sinners. I was still partaking in the worst of habits and life styles. I was still involved with drug dealers and gangsters. As the years rushed by, I had become the most unstable person I have ever known: "Madness, shame, hurt, anxiety, addiction, alcoholism, pornography, crime, depression, hatred, anger, revenge, broken heartedness, miserable, sadness, loneliness, violence, sickness, wickedness, godlessness, theft, paranoia, cruelty, betrayal, drug dealing, fighting, racism, imprisonment, gangsterism, suicide." The fruits of been separated from God!

I did not know, or rather I did not understand that the devil and his agents were warring against me. I did not know that their objective was to kill me and throw me into eternal misery! They very much succeeded. Six years had passed since I was released from prison. Suddenly I found myself in "a thousand pieces." I was a broken man. I was tired of crime. Tired of hurting people. Tired of life! I had now come to the end of myself. There was just nothing left in me. Nothing! Finally, I had a revolver stuck in my mouth. I know it sounds very weak of me, but what am I without The Lord as my strength? How terrible to be caught up in wickedness! I didn't want to live anymore, but I was too afraid of dying. I was so scared of pulling the trigger. In my hour of need, as I sat all alone in my empty room, my life flashing before me, I cried out in desperation to Jesus to help me. By the Mercy of our KING, the Power of our Risen Savior, the Goodness of our Creator and by His Infinite Love and Compassion, after calling upon The Name above every other Name, The Name of JESUS CHRIST, God made me put that gun away, and led me to a preacher who introduced me to Jesus Christ, The Messiah from Nazareth. And then, Mercy rewrote my life. God allowed me to repent before Him of all my filthy sins, and declared with my mouth, Jesus my Creator, King and God. The Lord God Almighty touched me right there and then, and I was set free from the powers of darkness, and every other thing that kept me in bondage. My chains were gone. Weeks later I was baptized. And I have never been the same since that moment in time.

For the next two years, I was literally shouting from the roof tops what Jesus had done for me. The desire in me was to give every drug addict, every drug dealer, every gangster, every other broken person the same divine opportunity as I had received, to meet Jesus, and to experience His healing power and life changing mercies. After two years of travelling the N1 highway, preaching in different towns, on the streets, in gang yards, in schools, and at jails, God led me to Mossel Bay. There I met Christa, who I am now married to. My lonely days had suddenly come to an end, and my broken heart was finally mended. We have a son named Samuel. He was born on the 1st of April 2013. Both Christa and Samuel are a gift from God to me, and to this ministry.

I focus on one thing: *Forgetting the past and looking forward to what lies ahead, I press on to reach the end of the race and receive the heavenly prize for which God, through Christ Jesus, is calling us.* - (PHILIPPIANS 3:13,14)

SIN AND REPENTANCE

Dreadful is the nature of sin! It, and nothing else renders us miserable, and separates us from God!

Every day you and I are travelling through this world toward eternity. To a destiny that will never end, and which cannot be changed once we arrive there. There are but two roads. Two destinations.

You are either on the road that leads to Heaven, or you are on the road of destruction that leads to hell. Do you know where you are going?

THE ROAD TO HELL

There are many people on this road. "The gate to hell is wide and the road that leads to it is easy, and there be many who travel it." (Matthew 7:13). Most of these people have their eyes closed. They do not know, and many don´;t care that they are on the road of destruction. "The evil god (the devil) of this world, has blinded their minds, who do not believe, lest the light of the gospel of the glory of Christ, who is the image of God, should shine on them." (2 Corinthians 4:4)

satan is a deceiver; Jesus described his true character when He called him "the father of lies." Jesus said; "he was a murderer from the beginning, and does not stand in the truth, because there is no truth in him. Whenever he speaks a lie, he speaks from his own nature; for he is a liar, and the father of lies" (John 8:44)

Just as Jesus manifests the truth speaks the truth and is the full embodiment of truth, satan manifests deception speaks lies and is the full embodiment of all that is false.

Throughout the ages, his objective has been to hinder man from knowing the truth. As the "god of this world," he has the ability to "blind" the minds of unbelievers from receiving the truth. He tempts and lures them to sin, and the deceitfulness of sin hinders them from seeing the truth of the gospel of Jesus Christ. Once he has blinded their minds, he is able to take them captive to do his will. And his will is for man to sin against God. The devil′;s will and purpose for man is to live in sin, and to die in sin. He wants to kill you and defeat you.

The road to hell is filled with people who have become so hardened to sin around them that they no longer fall on their faces before God and cry out for His mercy. They are bound in chains of darkness. They have become so hardened to sin that they fail to see the sins they allow to remain in their hearts they are unwilling to receive correction and reproof they are unrepentant.

They know God, but do not glorify Him. Their imaginations are unwholesome. Their foolish hearts are darkened. They boast of wisdom, yet, their hearts are foolish. They have fallen into idolatry, worshiping things created rather than the Creator. They have seperated themselves from God, fulfilling their lusts, dishonoring their bodies leading to a long list of sinful acts, which greatly displease God.

"And ever as they did not like to retain God in their knowledge, God gave them over to a reprobate mind, to do those things which are not convenient; Being filled with all unrighteousness, fornication, wickedness, covetousness, maliciousness; full of envy, murder, debate, deceit, malignity, whisperers. Backbiters, haters of God, despiteful, proud, boasters, inventors of evil things, disobedient to parents,. Without understanding, covenant breakers, without natural affection, implaceable, unmerciful. Who knowing the judgments of God, that they which commit such things are worthy of death, not only do the same, but have pleasure in them that do them." (Romans 1:28-32)

"Everyone has sinned, and come short of the glory of God (is far away from God′;s saving presence."Romans 3:23) You and I cannot get rid of a single sin by our own efforts. The load gets heavier as time goes on, and "Sin pays its wage-death." (Romans 6:23)

We cannot even hide one sin from God. "Man looks at the outward appearance, but God looks at the heart. "(1Samuel 16:7)

"Everyone must die once, and then after that be judged by God." (Hebrews 9:27) "Then I saw a great white throne and the one who sits on it And I saw the dead, great and small alike, standing before the throne. Books were opened, and then another book was opened, the book of the living. The dead were judged according to what they had done, as recorded in the books Whoever did not have his name written in the book of the living was thrown into the lake of fire." (Into Hell) (Revelation 20:11,12,15)

God';s Word tells us that there is a hell, a place of eternal punishment for those who do not obey God. The Word tells us that there is a hell for those who choose to hold the hand of satan and walk the road to hell. The Bible says, "They are going to end up in hell (whose end is destruction) because their god is their bodily desires, whose glory is their shame, who mind only the things of this world." (Phillipians 3:19)

But God is also a God of love, "He does not want anyone to be destroyed, but wants all to turn from their sins." (2 Peter 3:9) In His great kindness and love, He has made a way of escape for all who really want it. Do you want to find the way of life which leads to heaven?

THE WAY OF LIFE

Since we could not free ourselves from our sins, nor from the just punishment for our sins, God has provided a Saviour.

There is only one way to heaven.

Jesus said; "I Am The Way, the truth, and the life; no one comes to the Father except by me." (John 14:6) "Salvation is to be found through Him alone; in all the world there is no one else whom God has given who can save us." (Acts 4:12)

How Can We Start The Way of Life. The Way To Heaven?

"Repent, for The Kingdom of heaven is at hand!" (John 3:1-2)

Repentance is a descision that results in a change of mind, which in turn leads to a change of purpose and action.

There is no birth into the Kingdom without hearing the call to salvation, renouncing ones sin, and turning from sin towards Christ The Saviour. (Acts 3:19)

We all need to repent, even the "so-called" good people. "No-one is good, except God alone." (Mark10:18)

We can only enter this wonderful state "the way to heaven" through repentance and conversion and through accepting Jesus in faith. He makes us children of God. To repent, is the beginning of God´;s will for us.

Without repentance there is no forgiveness of sins. We remain dead in trespasses and sin! We remain on the road to hell! As The Father said about His lost son; This son of mine was dead and is alive again; he was lost and is found! So they began to celebrate: but the son repented and said to his Father; (Luke 15:21) "Father I have sinned against heaven and against you; I am not worthy to be called your son!" The confession of sin and his turning back to the house of his Father, was necessary for the prodical son to receive the full forgiveness of his sins.

Jesus said; " The time is fulfilled, and the Kingdom of God is at hand: repent, turn away from your sins and believe the Good News." (Mark 1:15)

Come to The Lord Jesus Christ, in prayer, just as you are with your load of sin, and ask Him to forgive you. He says, "I will never turn away anyone who comes to me." (John 6:37). "Come to me, all of you who are heavy burdened, and I will give you rest." (Matthew 11:28) Believe in Jesus alone for your deliverance from sin. "The Blood of Jesus, His Son, purifies us from every sin." (1 John 1:7)

He will give you a new life eternal life. Jesus said "Whoever hears My Words and believes in Him who sent Me has eternal life." "He will not be judged, but has already passed from death to life." (John 5:24). "When anyone is joined to Christ, he is a new creature (being); the old is gone, behold, the new has come." (2 Corinthians 5:17)

You will have peace in your heart. "Now that we have been put right with God through faith, we have peace with God through our Lord Jesus Christ." (Romans 5:1) "The testimony is this: God has given us eternal life, and this life has its source in His Son. Whoever has The Son has this life; whoever does not have The Son of God does not have life. I am writing to you so that you may KNOW that you have eternal life. You that believe in The Son of God." (1 John 5:11-13)

Jesus wants you to cast all your cares upon Him for He cares for you. (1 Peter 5:7) You can do this with the assurance that ..God has promised to supply all your needs according to His riches in Christ Jesus (Philippians 4:19). God will deliver you out of satans grasp (Psalm 91:3)

"That if thou shalt confess with thy mouth the Lord Jesus, and shalt believe in thine heart that God hath raised Him from the dead, thou shalt be saved. " (Romans 10:9)

And right now, if you have never given your heart to Jesus Christ, or never had a relationship with Him, then now is your hour.

Jesus Christ being the King of kings and The Lord of lords, He came down to this earth, and he went to the cross and He bore what we deserve on the cross, because of His love for us, and now, he offers it for free to you. If you have never made Him Lord of your life, make that commitment right now. Don´;t walk away without saying Lord Jesus I need you. Don´;t walk away without taking hold of Jesus. Make sure that you going to heaven. Be sure that Jesus has saved you. Be sure that you are born again.

The hope of eternity in Heaven with Jesus, no more tears, no more sorrow, no more pain, no more hell. And even right now, you can have Jesus walk with you every other day of your life as He prepares you for eternity.

WHAT TO PRAY: (SINNERS PRAYER)

Lord Jesus, I am a sinner and I need You.

I repent of my sin. Please forgive me. Please save me.

I believe You shed Your Blood for me, and died for me.

I believe God raised You from the dead.

I choose to walk away from my sin.

I invite You to come and live in my heart as my personal Saviour.

Thank You that I am Your child. Amen

If you have prayed the sinners prayer, and have accepted Jesus as your Lord and Saviour, then you have just begun a wonderful new life with Him. YOU ARE SET FREE!

"That the house of Israel may go no more astray from me, neither be polluted any more with all their transgressions; but that they may be My people, and I may be their God, saith The Lord GOD." (Ezekiel 14:11)

God has established an everlasting covenant with you and has sealed it with His oath that He will never break it. You are now a new part of a new nation; God´;s spiritual Israel. GOD is now your GOD, and you are part of His covenant people. By repenting and making Jesus Lord of your life, God has taken possession of you. By His Spirit He has circumsiced your heart, taken out the stony heart, and has given you a heart filled with His love.

He has restored our will and brought it into perfect harmony with His Will, so that you now have a desire to LOVE Him with your whole heart.

He has given you the power to obey Him and keep His commandments.

He has forgiven all your sins, blotted them out and given you power over sin.

As your God, He has made you one with Him. He has given you His glory .all that He is and has.

In this blood-covenant relationship, Jesus has "given to you ALL things that pertain unto life and Godliness" (2 Peter 1:3). Jesus has given you "exceeding great and precious promises" and has made you "partaker of the divine nature" (2 Peter1:4)

You are set free from the bondage of sin. You have been called to freedom. Under the new covenant you have been called to walk in the freedom of the Spirit. It is through faith in the work Jesus accomplished on Calvary that you have entered into a blood-covenant relationship with God. By faith, you must stand fast in the liberty wherewith Jesus has made you free, and not be entangled again with the yoke of bondage (Galatians 5:1)

To walk in freedom, you must be led by The Spirit of God. You must no longer depend upon your own strength, but upon the power of The Holy Spirit. Paul told the Galatians; "But I say, walk and live habitually in the (Holy) Spirit-responsive to and controlled and guided by The Spirit; then you will certainly not gratify the cravings and desires of the flesh But if you are guided (led) by The (Holy) Spirit you are not subject to the Law" (Galatians 5:16,18)

You have been saved and set free to walk in 100 percent obedience to God. To obtain the promise under the new covenant, you must be obedient to God. You must be responsive to His voice and the leading of The Holy Spirit.

Refuse to listen to those who say it is impossible to walk in perfect obedience to God. It is impossible to walk in obedience to God in our limited strength (in the flesh); but, it is possible through the power of The Holy Spirit Who lives within us!

"For Sin Shall Not (any longer) Exert Dominion Over You, Since Now You Are Not Under Law (as slaves), But Under Grace As Subjects Of God´;s Favor And

Mercy" (Romans 6:14)

You have been set free from the power of the flesh! Paul said; "For the Law of the Spirit of life (Which is) Christ Jesus (the law of our new being), has freed me from the law of sin and of death. For God has done what the Law could not do, (its power) being weakened by the flesh (that is, the entire nature of man without The Holy Spirit). Sending His Own Son in the guise of sinful flesh and as an offering for sin, (God) condemned sin in the flesh, subdued, overcame, deprived it of its power (over all who accept that sacrifice). So that the righteous and just requirement of the Law might be fully met in us, who live and move not in the ways of the flesh but in the ways of The Spirit, our lives governed not by the standards and according to the dictates of the flesh, but controlled by the (Holy) Spirit" (Romans 8:2-4)

Here are some guide lines of how to live your new life with Jesus.

HOW TO LIVE THE NEW LIFE

1. Read The Bible every day: Besides been a light for our way; it is food for the soul. "Be like new-born babies, always thirsty for the pure spiritual milk, so that by drinking it you may grow up." (1 Peter 2:2) Ask God to guide you and teach you by His Holy Spirit, as you read.

2. Come near to God in prayer every day, praying in the Name of Jesus. "Don';t worry about anything, but in all your prayers ask God for what you need, always asking Him with a thankful heart. And God's peace, which is far beyond human understanding, will keep your hearts and minds safe in union with Christ Jesus." (Phillipians 4:6-7)

3. Speak to others about Jesus. "Go back to your family and tell them how much The Lord has done for you and how kind He has been to you." (Mark 5:19)

4. In temptation call upon The Lord. "He can help those who are tempted, because He Himself was temted and suffered." (Hebrews 2:18)

5. If you do sin again, confess it quickly to God. "But if we confess our sins to God, He will keep His promise and do what is right: He will forgive us our sins and purify us from wrongdoing." (1 John 1:9)

6. Try to associate with other believers in The Lord Jesus Christ, where the Bible is the final authority "My commandment is this: love one another, just as I have loved you." (John 15:12)

7. Always obey God. "Whoever loves Me will obey my teaching." (John 14:23)

8. Do not be afraid, for Christ is with you. "I will never leave you; I will never forsake you." (Hebrews 13:5)

9. Be Baptized. "Then Peter said unto them, Repent, and be baptized everyone of you in The Name of Jesus Christ for the remission of sins, and ye shall receive the gift of The Holy Ghost." (Acts 2:38) "He that believeth and is baptized shall be saved.."(Mark 16:16) "Let us draw near with a true heart in full assurance of faith, having our hearts sprinkled from an evil concience, and our bodies washed in pure water." (Hebrews 10:22)

10. Give yourself completely to The Lord Jesus Christ. Let Him direct your life according to His Will. In this you be completely free and find true happiness in Him. "And thy shall love The Lord thy God with all thine heart, and with all thy soul, and with all thy might." (Deuteronomy 6:5)

Stay by His feet my friend. Jesus Loves you. You are saved and free. Never look back and long for the old life ..that dirty old road which is filled with sin and death.

William Austen

www.ingramcontent.com/pod-product-compliance
Lightning Source LLC
Chambersburg PA
CBHW072100110526
44590CB00018B/3257